Endorsements

This book takes over where the Twelve Steps leave off. Charles Whitfield skillfully explains the connections between the Twelve Steps and the spirituality of A Course in Miracles and the growth we can have beyond Twelve Step work.

Jack C., Twelve Step Fellowship Member

A Course in Miracles comes from the same intelligence that we visited in our Near-death experience. This book clearly summarizes much of that.

Jane S., Near-death experiencer

Charles Whitfield takes us into the heart and soul of A Course in Miracles. This book is an excellent companion to reading the Course itself. ...Highly recommended.

Jyoti and Russell Park, PhD
Center for Sacred Studies, California

I had heard of A Course in Miracles but never had time to read it. I eventually got a copy of it and started reading but couldn't get into it. This book helped me finally open it again, and even more, to understand many of its main messages.

Stephen Mitchell, Fine Arts Director, Private School

On The Cover

On the cover is the center of a 120-year-old stained glass window that I rescued from an old church being remodeled. It shows a white dove -- an ancient symbol of the Holy Spirit. Although I had read *A Course in Miracles* since the late l970's, some 12 years before we met, in 1991 Barbara and I began reading it together. Every morning after breakfast we walked beneath this full stained glass window, sat on our sun porch and read a lesson or a section from it.

Sometime later, Barbara said, "My past near-death experience had given me an understanding that I'd never been able to articulate before, and now, here it was, in this book. We can think somewhat as God by creating our shift in perception through forgiveness. In that forgiveness, we let go of our false self or ego and energize our True Self, who we really are."

"One morning I went to the porch, thinking that I would pick up the Course and read it again. As I reached out for it, I was thinking that this book shows us the Holy Spirit. As my hand touched the book, I was startled by a loud thud on the almost all-glass door. I looked up, and saw that a dove had smacked into the window. As it shook out its feathers the dove and I had eye contact. Within a few seconds it flew away. Charlie came in and together we noticed the abstract but beautiful imprint of the dove's head, eye, beak, wings and body that it had left on the glass, and he took several pictures of the left imprint, one of which we show on page 131 after the Appendix."

Choosing God

A Bird's Eye View of *A Course in Miracles*

For — Spiritual Seekers,

People in Recovery,

those in Twelve Step fellowships,

Near-death Experiencers,

Agnostics, Atheists,

and

the Religiously and Spiritually Curious

Charles L Whitfield, MD

Author of *Healing The Child Within* and *The Power of Humility*

MHP

muse house press

Muse House Press
ISBN: 978-1-935827-00-9

Trade Paperback

Requests for information and rights should be addressed to:

Muse House Press

Find us on the Internet at:

www.MuseHousePress.com

www.cbwhit.com

www.BarbaraWhitfield.com

Muse House Press and the MHP Logo are imprints of Muse House Press.

Cover design and Interior composition by:

Donald Brennan / YakRider Media

Updated Edition 2014

Printed in the United States of America

ACKNOWLEDGMENTS

Grateful thanks and acknowledgment for permission to use or quote material from the following sources:

To Kenneth Wapnick for his several identified quotes and for permission to reproduce his Chart 1 from his 1990 book *A Vast Illusion: Time according to ACIM*.

To Robert Perry for permission for me to summarize some of his work on the Course, including his review of the evolution of the Course versions in a scholarly article on his website: www.circleofa.org.

To Allen Watson for permission to reproduce his Chart of The Journey Home from his 1994 book The Journey Home.

To my wife Barbara for her help typing the manuscript and our ongoing studying the Course together and individually.

To Donald Brennan for his excellent layout and graphic design of this book.

To my many other colleagues, some cited in the references here, who write and teach about the Course for their continued inspiration, and to the members of the Board of the Foundation for Inner Peace for their unselfish giving of the Course to us.

To Alcoholics Anonymous for permission to reproduce its Twelve Steps

And to Helen Schucman and Bill Thetford for receiving *A Course in Miracles* and sharing it with us all with the editorial assistance of Kenneth Wapnick and the publishing assistance of Judy Skutch Whitson of the Foundation for Inner Peace; and to the latter two for permission to reproduce photos from the archives of ACIM and the DVD Memories of Helen & Bill.

Dedication

For — **Spiritual Seekers,**

People in Recovery,

those in Twelve Step fellowships,

Near-death Experiencers,

Agnostics, Atheists,

and

the **Religiously** and **Spiritually Curious**

Table of Contents

Tables

Maps

Figures

Charts

Using References to the Course in This Book

I use a more reader-friendly reference method than most writers on the Course. For example, for a quote's reference code of **67T, 1:6** the **67** denotes the **page number** in the Course, **T** indicates that it is in the **Text** volume of the Course, **1** means the **paragraph on that page,** and **6** means the **sentence** of that paragraph, as numbered in the recent editions of ACIM.

T = **Text**
W = **Workbook**
M = **Manual for Teachers**
P = **Psychotherapy**
S = **Song of Prayer**
C = **Clarification of Terms** (at end of Manual for Teachers)

A
COURSE
IN
MIRACLES
COMBINED VOLUME
PREFACE
TEXT
WORKBOOK FOR STUDENTS
MANUAL FOR TEACHERS
CLARIFICATION OF TERMS
SUPPLEMENTS
FOUNDATION FOR INNER PEACE

PREFACE

A *Course in Miracles* is the most spiritually exciting book I have ever read. I have found no other spiritual writing as intellectually stimulating, yet so practical in our relationships with ourself, others and God.

Do you want peace or pain? If you want peace, the Course suggests, "Choose God." It's that simple. What is not so simple is knowing exactly why, when and how to choose God. The Course provides answer after answer to these questions and more. And it gives us ongoing psychological nourishment.

A major focus of the Course is on the process of forgiveness by letting go of our ego. But over the last century the ego has been more misunderstood than clear. The Course makes our understanding of the ego as clear as I have ever seen it, which makes it easier to let it go.

People in the forefront of psychology and relationships have long realized the need for a bridge between psychology and spirituality. The Course provides that bridge. I have long observed my patients getting better by adding spirituality to their program of recovery. I have also seen numerous people in Twelve Step programs use the Course to expand and continue their Twelve Step work.

I have used the Course personally as spiritual nourishment for over 30 years, and it has enriched all of my relationships. For eight years, my wife Barbara and I have read a section from it to one another most mornings after breakfast. We have also taught its principles together. I especially like that the Course is a private and personal exchange between me and its author. There is no other authority figure imposing itself between me and what he is saying.

This book is an **introduction** to and a **bird's eye view** of the Course. It starts slowly and gradually builds to provide an explanation for its major teachings. I have used it in the classes I teach on spirituality in general and on the Course in particular here in Atlanta and across the country, including at the Rutgers University Summer School of Alcohol and Drug Studies.

While it may provide a clear and useful overview of its major teachings, this book is **not** intended to be **a substitute for reading and studying the Course**. To get its full meaning and message, I recommend that anyone stimulated by this or any other book that addresses it get a copy of the Course and read it regularly. There is no substitute for the real words.

With that said, I hope that this book and its subsequent volume *Teachers of God*, will provide a useful guide to understanding the powerful and yet peaceful message of *A Course in Miracles.*

1 Introduction to the Course

A Course in Miracles is a modern spiritual text that was published in 1975-76 in three volumes, consisting of a *Text*, a *Workbook for Students*, and a *Manual for Teachers*. Since then an increasing number of spiritual seekers, including people in recovery from all sorts of pain, problems and disorders, are beginning to read and study the Course. At the same time, some have found it to be complex and difficult to grasp. Because of this increasing interest - yet some difficulty understanding it, it may be useful for any of them, as well as their helping professionals, Twelve Step sponsors, friends and family to know some of what the Course says.

The Course has no religious affiliation, being a universal curriculum for learning effective spiritual principles. Although it has a clearly Christian tone and content, people from diverse faiths have studied and used it to enrich their lives. Indeed, three of the four core people who brought the Course into existence and publication came from a Jewish background.

The Course is a gentle and loving description of what may be some answers to the four perennial questions, Who am I? What am I doing here? Where am I going? How can I get any peace? It reframes, re-interprets and expands traditional Judeo-Christian understandings into perhaps a more palatable presentation for many of its readers. While it is also compatible with a universal spirituality that may include some Eastern religious principles, the Course says that it is but one of thousands of spiritual paths, and thus may not be for everyone.

If a person decides to read it, the Course says little about how or in what order to do it, i.e., what book or section one should read first, and so on. One way is to begin reading one workbook lesson daily, while also beginning to sample or read the Text and/or the Teacher's Manual. I have been reading the Course since the late l970's and still find it to be spiritually nourishing, no matter what part I read.

How It Came

In the late 1960's and early 1970's the Course was scribed over a seven year period by a non-religious PhD psychology researcher named Helen Schucman who worked as a psychology professor at Columbia University College of Physicians and Surgeons. She and her boss, Bill Thetford PhD, had worked together for several years and had noticed their frequent conflicts and tensions with others at Columbia and with each other. One day Bill said to Helen, "There must be a better way" to handle all this conflict and stress, and Helen surprised Bill by agreeing and saying that she would support their looking for a better way.

A few months later Helen began to have some memorable dreams with spiritual content and then in 1965 she heard a voice that said to her, "This is a course in miracles. Please take notes." Upset, she called Bill, who listened to her and then said he would read any notes she took the next morning with her privately. They were both interested enough for Helen to transcribe what the voice told her and for Bill to type what she had written daily over the following seven years.

Helen and psychologist Ken Wapnick PhD eventually organized the Course into chapters, sections and paragraphs by and with Judy Skutch and some of their colleagues published it in the three volumes. (To get some of the full story of how it came, I suggest reading *Journey Without Distance*: The Story of ACIM, by Robert Skutch and/or *Absence from Felicity* by Ken Wapnick. For those who would like a faster presentation, The Foundation for Inner Peace, which publishes the Course, produced a 2 1/4 hour videotape and DVD called "The Story of A Course in Miracles," available from some libraries, Unity Churches, and new age bookstores (for about $60). The jacket on the videotape says:

"A Course in Miracles is a three volume set of books, a self study course designed to help change one's perceptions. Often referred to as a metaphysical system of spiritual psychotherapy, it was

taken down between 1965 and 1972 by Dr. Helen Schucman, a highly respected research psychologist, who heard a 'voice' dictating the material to her. Throughout the entire project she was given assistance and support by Dr. William N. Thetford, a professor of medical psychology at Columbia University's College of Physicians and Surgeons." (The ACIM website says that there are more than a million copies of the Course in circulation worldwide [with nearly 2 million as of today]. The Course has been translated into 18 other languages.)

The first half of this memorable two hour-film, *The Forgotten Song,* is the extraordinary story of how the Course came to be. This definitive documentary, featuring Dr. Thetford, and filmed on location, spans a seventy-year period in the life of Helen Schucman, and includes dramatized segments of some of the psycho-spiritual visions and dreams that led up to the actual scribing' of the Course. Helen's own words, from her unpublished autobiography, are clearly spoken by actress Glynis Johns. *The Song Remembered,* the second half of the film, contains firsthand accounts of 27 students of the Course who tell what the material means to them, and how it has affected their lives. Included are psychologists, educators, physicians, business people, prison inmates and others.

KEN WAPNICK PHD, BILL THETFORD PHD, HELEN SCHUCMAN PHD, AND JUDY SKUTCH WHITSON

WHO AM I? A MAP OF THE MIND

The *Introduction* to the Course says,

"This is a course in miracles. It is a required course. Only the time you take it is voluntary. Free will does not mean that you can establish the curriculum. It means only that you can elect what you want to take at a given time. The course does not aim at teaching the meaning of love, for that is beyond what can be taught. It does aim, however, at removing the blocks to the awareness of love's presence, which is your natural inheritance. The opposite of love is fear, but what is all-encompassing can have no opposite.

This course can therefore be summed up very simply in this way:

Nothing real can be threatened.
Nothing unreal exists.
Herein lies the peace of God.

Where it says "Nothing real can be threatened," I understand that what is *real* is God and God's world. This is in contrast to the ego and its world, which is *unreal*, and which according to the Course does not exist.

What is God and God's world? I don't exactly know. Here is a map of the psyche that may help us better understand the Course that I have found useful that might begin to describe the Divine Mystery and how we fit into God's world. While the map is not the territory, maps can be useful.

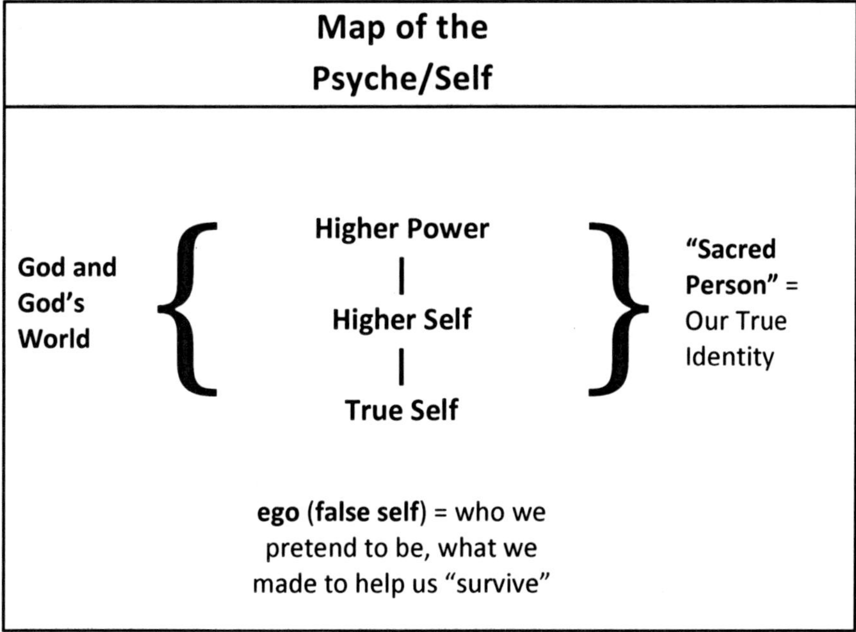

Other names for the True Self, who I really am, include the real or existential self, the human heart, the soul and the Child Within. They are all the same and they are our true identity. I also have within me a divine nature, sometimes called a guardian angel, Atman, Buddha Nature, Christ Consciousness, Higher Self or simply Self. And both of these -- my True Self and my Higher Self -- are intimately connected to my Higher Power, God/Goddess/All-That-Is, a part of which is also within me.

I see this relationship - True Self, Higher Self and Higher Power - as being such an important relationship that I can also view it as being one Person, which I call the *Sacred Person*. As a part of the Mystery, my True Self makes or constructs an assistant to help me as I live out this human experience. We can call this assistant, this sidekick, the *ego* - also known as the *false self* or co-dependent self. When the ego is helpful to us, such as in screening, sorting and handling many aspects of our internal and external reality, we can call it positive ego. But as Lazaris describes, when it tries to take over and run our life, it becomes negative ego. While it does not use the term "negative" the Course focuses on negative ego and how to transcend it.

In my view, this map of the psyche is more evolved than the maps of Freud, Jung and their colleagues of up to 100 years ago, when they used the term "ego" to mean both True Self and false self. Since the 1930's we have begun to make this more precise differentiation between True Self and false self, and today we can most accurately use "ego" as being synonymous with the false self. In Chapter 14 I show a more expanded map that is taken from my understanding of some of the terms used in the Course. While this above map is not taken directly from the Course, I and the people we have taught have found that it forms a base upon which we can understand the Course more easily.

What is real is God and God's world, that of the Sacred Person. The Course says that the ego and its world are not real, and therefore, in the grand scheme of the Mystery, do not exist. Herein, when we make this differentiation, lies our peace and serenity.

2 Miracles and Relationships

While what follows is too simplified to describe the full content and message of the Course, it may provide a new reader with an overview of what it says, as well as provide a review and possibly even a new perspective for a reader who is already familiar with it.

According to the Course, a miracle is not an event, like feeding a multitude with one loaf or raising the dead. Rather, it is an *experience* that occurs when we choose God over our ego. And it is much more. To better understand its healing experience, in the next few paragraphs I will summarize some of its basic principles that I have learned from reading the Course since 1977 and from the work of two of the Course's master teachers Robert Perry and Ken Wapnick.[1]

Background

Much of what follows is "heady" or somewhat dry material and is in some ways different from some common religious understandings. Yet most readers of the Course find its contents to be liberating psychologically and spiritually. So bear with me in this chapter while I summarize some of the Course's essential principles about relationships. After this chapter the material expands and offers a more lively and powerful healing psychology and spirituality. If you find this material is too ponderous, consider skipping to the next chapter.

A main message of the Course is a special kind of letting go that it calls *forgiveness*, which is actually letting go of our ego, that is a major block to

---

[1] While Perry and Wapnick see the Course mostly similarly, they have a few differences reflected in their writings and teachings, as summarized in the website: www.circleofa.org/articles/BigPicture.php

our experience of God. The ego is a belief that we have about ourselves that we are separated from others and from God, and are completely on our own (e.g., see 67T, 1:6) - here 67 denotes the page number in the Course, T indicates the Text volume of the Course, 1 means the paragraph on that page and 6 means the sentence of that paragraph, as numbered in the recent edition of ACIM. See also 58T, 8:1-4.

The way we let go of our ego (and the emotional pain that it continually generates within us) is that - whenever we are not at peace – we can choose God. The Course says that whenever we are not feeling peace that we can remember to choose God over our ego. I have found that we can do so most readily in this regard by saying a simple one word prayer: "Help."

The Course says that the ego is composed of what it calls the "unholy trinity" of sin, guilt and fear. It describes *Sin* as our belief in separation, *Guilt* as all of our painful feelings and beliefs, and says that our *Fear* results because we believe that we deserve God's punishment, since we think that by separating from God we have hurt or rejected God.

Special Relationships

Through our ego and its unholy trinity we turn God into our adversary or enemy, and then in a vicious cycle turn back to our ego for protection (66T, 4:7). Our ego says "I'll save you" by two ways. First, deny or repress your guilt and fear.[2] If doing that doesn't work, then *project* your guilt and fear *onto others*. We can so project our pain in what the Course

---

[2] The Course describes guilt as what therapists and counselors know more as *shame* (which is about 80% of what the Course means when it refers to guilt, with the remaining 20% being what we understand as guilt.

calls *special* relationships. It describes two kinds: 1) the special ***hate*** relationship, through attack, hate, resentment, or prejudice, and 2) the special ***love*** relationship. In the special love relationship, I say "I love you," and if you love me the way I want, you will complete me. When you don't, I attack. The special love relationship uses *conditional* love, and is in part what we have called "co-dependence" (Whitfield 1997).

In both of these kinds of special relationships I say, through my ego, "You've taken away my peace," and the more I attack, the more guilt and shame I feel. Based on my reading of the Course and on Wapnick's 1978 booklet "Christian Psychology in *A Course in Miracles*," I have summarized some of the main characteristics of these two kinds of special relationships as follows (Whitfield 1992, 97).

The Special Relationship

1. **Denies the need for relationship with or assistance from God.**

2. **Is based on self-hate from guilt and shame.**

3. **Hides this shame and guilt under the guise of love or hate of another.**

4. **Thus places the answer to our shame/guilt outside of us.**

5. **Assumes that something is lacking in us and that we need it to be happy.**

6. **Fixes expectations on the other (i.e., the special relationship). By so doing, it denies the other's true identity in God (i.e., that they are a part of God).**

7. **Is based on the "scarcity principle," that there is**

only a limited amount of love to go around.

8. **Becomes the focus of our anger and resentments.**

9. **Shifts responsibility for our happiness to the other (i.e., the special relationship). For example, "If only you were or would be such and such, then I would be happy."**

10. **The ego (false or co-dependent self) uses the special relationship for attacking the other by projecting our shame and guilt onto the other and thus promising salvation (i.e., happiness and fulfillment).**

If many relationships are this way, how can they ever work? The Course's answer is that we do not have to control more by trying to be or do something that we are not (our ego), e.g., by doing more, better or different, which our ego wants. Rather, all we need is a "little willingness" to open ourself to the healing power of God, which it refers to as "the awareness of Love's presence," among other terms. When we do so, a miracle happens. We shift our perception by choosing God (which the Course calls *right mind*) over our ego (*wrong mind*), and we heal.

We simply shift our way of thinking. We change our mind about our mind. What results is a ***process*** that continues as the Course's answer to the special relationship, which it calls a *Holy Relationship*, summarized as follows.

THE HOLY RELATIONSHIP

1. **Based on my love of God and True Self/Higher Self.**

2. **I see this love in everyone.**

3. **I take responsibility for my suffering by looking within myself.**

4. **I address and release my shame, guilt, hurt, anger, and resentment through miracles and the forgiveness process.**

5. **I realize that there is only abundance of Love, and that the scarcity principle is only an illusion.**

6. **I know that there is nothing lacking in me, that I am a perfect child of God, and that my natural state is peace and serenity.**

7. **I respect my [positive] ego (Lazaris 1980) and use it as an assistant in my growth.**

8. **To facilitate this experience, I use daily spiritual practice.**

9. **I live and relate in the present moment, the Now (i.e., the Holy Instant).**

10. **In relationships I am open and communicating, trusting, kind, gentle, peaceful, joyful and celebrating.**

These characteristics of a Holy Relationship are also those of a healthy relationship, which includes a balance of healthy dependence and healthy independence. They are compatible with Twelve Step programs and with the core teachings of the world's great religious systems, both eastern and western.

I assisted a couple in their late 40's who had repeated and painful conflicts with each other for several years. Being adults who had grown up in troubled and dysfunctional families, both had worked for some time on those issues in a recovery program (which I describe as "Stage Two Recovery" later in Chapter 8.) They had also studied the Course alone and with one another for several years, and had often prayed for help with their conflicts. While their conflicts continued, they did show some improvement as they studied the Course and practiced its principles of miracles, forgiveness and letting go of their egos (which are about the same process and experience.) Their repeated conflicts had several characteristics of the special relationship, and as they healed, their increasing peace was a reflection of a holy relationship. Finally, one day they decided to pray together and ask the Holy Spirit to help them, which was followed by progressively more peace in their relationship.

THE PROBLEM AND THE ANSWER

The Course says that we have only one problem: separation. Through our imagined separation from God and from others, the ego believes we attacked God, who is angry at us for doing that and will therefore punish us. This illusion of the ego unfortunately leads to our feeling guilt/shame and fear, which we then often project onto others (Wapnick 1976, 85). To this single problem there is one answer: forgiveness, which is a shift in perception and experience that occurs when we choose God over our ego. This choosing and shift into feeling at peace is also the miracle.

3 Some Miracle Principles

On pages 3 through 6 of the *Text*, the Course lists 50 principles of miracles, including a brief discussion or explanation of some of them. The reader is then left to search through the rest of the *Text, Workbook* and *Teacher's Manual* cognitively, as well as experientially throughout their life, for how these miracles and their principles happen and how they feel. In the following sections I will comment on several of these miracle principles or their **characteristics**, which are identified in **boldface** type.

Shift in Perception

I mentioned above that a miracle is a **shift in perception** that happens when we **choose God** or God's Holy Spirit **over the ego**. This choosing then brings about a psychological and spiritual **correction in our thinking, feeling or behaving** that otherwise may be causing us conflict and pain. In this sense, the miracle is **healing** of the conflict and pain.

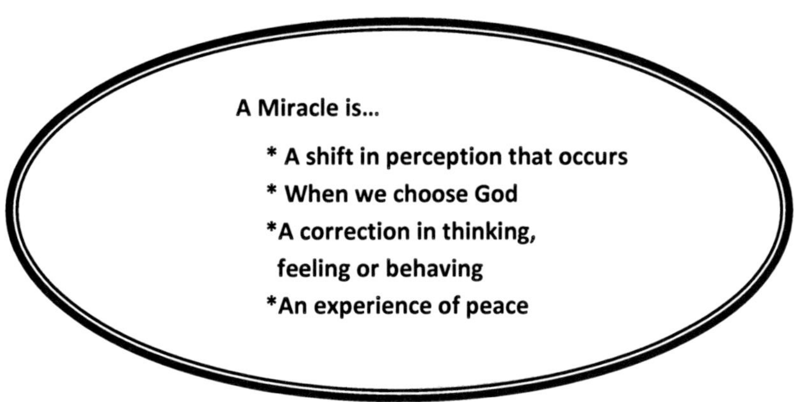

A Miracle is...
* A shift in perception that occurs
* When we choose God
*A correction in thinking, feeling or behaving
*An experience of peace

Miracles **happen naturally as expressions of love**. The miracle is a teaching and learning device for experiencing unity or Atonement, and thereby corrects and heals the separation (that never was). It teaches us that to give is to receive, so that when we give love we thereby receive it. In this sense, the giver is the receiver, the teacher is the pupil, the therapist/counselor is the patient/client, the parent is the child, and so on.

Miracles also teach that the **mind**, not the body, is the problem when it chooses wrongly. When our mind **chooses God**, the Holy Spirit and/or Christ, the Course calls it ***right*** *mind*, which is perhaps the closest term to the True or Real Self, or Child Within, that it uses. When it chooses the ego (or false self), it calls it *wrong mind*.

Miracles **transcend** several things, including the body and **all things physical**. This principle reminds me of Antoine de Saint Exupery's writing in *The Little Prince* when the fox said, "Remember, it is only with the heart that one can see rightly. What is essential is invisible to the eye." Written decades before the Course, these statements anticipate this miracle characteristic. Ken Wapnick (l985) added that miracles also transcend worldly laws (such as those related to biology, nutrition, friendship, religion, economics, stress, immunizations and death) - all of which are ego made or oriented.

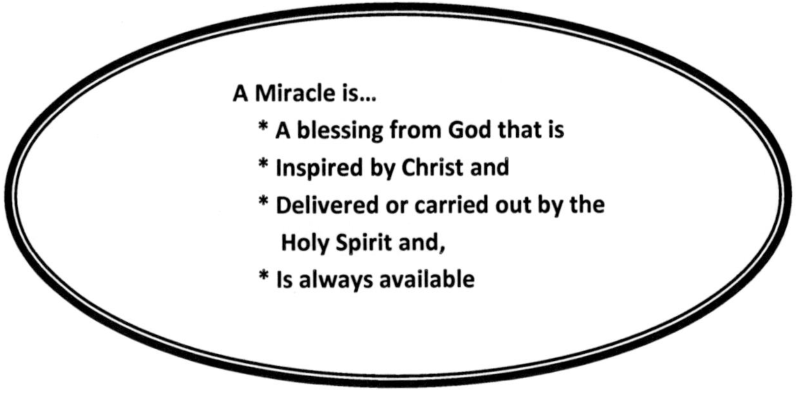

A Miracle is...
* A blessing from God that is
* Inspired by Christ and
* Delivered or carried out by the Holy Spirit and,
* Is always available

NATURAL SIGNS OF FORGIVENESS

Miracles are **never lost**, and are **a service** in that they affect others and are a way of loving our neighbor as ourself. In that sense, they are **natural signs of forgiveness**. They are a **correction for** how we **perceive or think** wrongly, which may then shift or change our behavior.

Principle number 25 says, "Miracles are part of an interlocking chain of forgiveness which, when completed, is the Atonement. Atonement works all the time and in all dimensions of time." While conventional Christianity sees atonement (of our sins) coming only through repentance, sacrifice and suffering, the Course describes *Atonement* as being the *correction* or *undoing* of believing the ego's error that we are separate, and thus is the undoing of fear.

Each time that **we forgive** others or ourself **by choosing God**/Holy Spirit/Christ over the ego, which is the miracle, **we add to the** chain or **Circle of Atonement**, discussed later (282T, 1-11). The Course says that our only task is to accept the Atonement for ourself. When we each do that, the overall plan of the Atonement is complete.

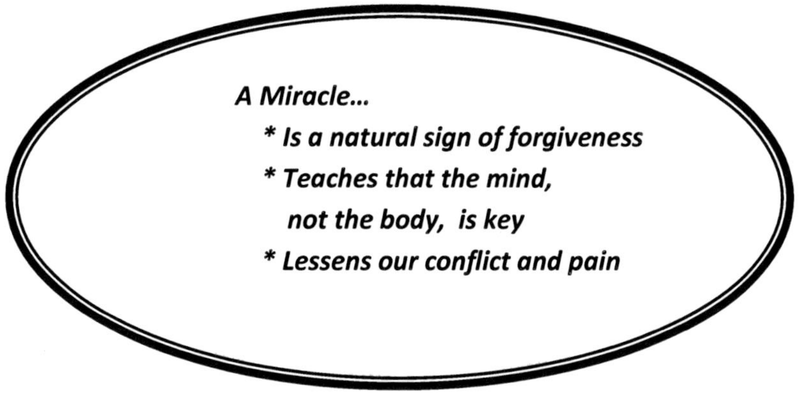

A Miracle...
* Is a natural sign of forgiveness
* Teaches that the mind,
not the body, is key
* Lessens our conflict and pain

Miracles **lessen** our painful feelings of **fear**, **guilt** and shame, and teach us that sin is a mistake that needs correction, not an inborn defect or behavior that has to be repented or punished. Miracles are universal **blessings** from God inspired through Christ to all of his brothers and sisters, and through them we reciprocally praise God. Miracles allow us to **look beyond** our differences, errors, mistakes, "sins", or egos to the **Christ** that resides and shines **within** each of us.

I have noticed that when I am in conflict and feel pain from it, that I can usually bring about a miracle. I pause, ask God (or Holy Spirit or Christ) for help, and within a few seconds or a few minutes I usually feel less pain and more peace. For me, that process and experience are what I understand to be a miracle. Sometimes that one miracle experience is enough to help my particular conflict. At other times I need to ask for help again, and sometimes several more times. But what is important to me is that my asking usually works. I've also noticed that once I've prayed, within a short or longer time something intervenes in my life that is more gentle, creative, and powerful in a healing way than anything I would have imagined. This choice for God and the ensuing experience of peace usually amazes and delights me.

Assist in Realizing Spirituality

Miracles **assist** us in experiencing our **spirituality** by placing Spirit at the center, and thereby also **inspire gratitude**. They teach and honor that **we are each holy** and **lovable**. They **bring us peace** and **restore our sanity** (which we also experience when we are in our right mind), and show that **we are not lacking** in anything. Miracles are **expressions of love**, and may touch people we have not met, so they **may have effects of which we are not aware.**

While **Christ inspires** miracles, the **Holy Spirit** is their **mechanism,** since He can see totally, rather than selectively. The Holy Spirit is a bridge that has "one foot" in Reality ("Heaven") and the other in the dream in which we have fallen asleep (Wapnick 1985). Holy Spirit **dissolves error** by seeing it as false or unreal, just as darkness disappears when light shines on it. The *extension* of the miracle or *what happens after it* (which is Atonement or forgiveness) *is not our concern*; rather that is the job of the Holy Spirit - once we have "turned it over" by so choosing God.

The Holy Spirit is the highest way of communicating, and miracles are **temporary ways** of **communicating.** When we return to direct revelation, which is our original form of communication with God, our need for miracles is over (Principle number 46). The experience of revelation unites us directly with God, and we feel God's presence, and that is also temporary. (After Chapter 1, revelation is mentioned in the Course only twice.)

Miracles correct our false perception of lack (i.e., the scarcity principle). Miracles arise from our being open to them, or miracle-ready, which is part of being in our right mind.

Learning Devices

Miracles are **learning devices** that **lessen our need for time**, and are the means that the Holy Spirit uses to teach us that we are not victims of the world. Finally, miracles **compare** what *we* make with (God's) Creation, **accepting** what is in accord with **creation** as true, and rejecting what is out of accord as false (Principle number 50). This is related to the closing lines in the Introduction to the Course, which says:

Nothing real can be threatened.
Nothing unreal exists.
Herein lies the peace of God.

A Miracle...

***Transcends the body and world**

*** Is a temporary way of communicating**

***Helps us learn and experience unity and the Atonement**

The above is but an overview of some of the main characteristics of the miracle principles. As for all of the material in this bird's eye view, I suggest that the reader look further at the Course itself for these 50 principles, which it lists on pages 3 through 6 and then elaborates upon them throughout its three volumes.

The ego seeks to divide and separate.
Spirit seeks to unify and heal.

A Course in Miracles, p 110 T

---

4 Similarities to the Twelve Steps

These miracle principles and the others described in the Course have many similarities to those reflected in the Twelve Steps of AA and other self-help fellowships. Having studied the Steps for over 40 years and the Course for over 30 years, I have noticed that the Course discusses and expands what the Steps address so efficiently. While it may use slightly different language or terms, the Course tells us more exactly how to do such things as "turn it over" and "let go and let God," as well as describes what God's Will is for us, and how to look at addictions and our ego. For ease of reference, I reproduce the Twelve Steps of AA on the next page (the bolded words are my emphasis on those that I consider key). ...Skip this chapter if you have no interest. I think they give us another practical correlation with the Course's message.

These Steps are the 214 most powerful and influential words I know. As I have reflected on similar aspects of the Steps and the Course, I have seen how closely they complement one another. They are not only entirely compatible, but are supportive of each other, with the Course providing perhaps more support just by its sheer volume and depth of spiritual information and nourishment. As an example of their mutual support, I briefly discuss one aspect of humility two pages below.

Both the Twelve Steps and the Course are spiritual programs of healing, and are not aligned with any sect or religion. At the same time, both do not say that they are the only spiritual path to healing. Both have no earthly leaders, have clear principles that are described in their texts, and say that only a little willingness is necessary to begin working their program of healing/recovery. Even so, it would be no surprise that some people will struggle with either or both of these paths, and that some may choose not to pursue them.

Both programs ...

***Are spiritual programs of healing**
***See ego as a major block**
***Are not aligned with any sect/religion**

THE TWELVE STEPS OF ALCOHOLICS ANONYMOUS

1. We admitted we were **powerless** over alcohol -- that our lives had become **unmanageable.**

2. **Came to believe** that a Power greater than ourselves **could restore** us to **sanity.**

3. Made a **decision** to **turn our will** and our **lives** over to the **care of God** as we understood Him.

4. Made a **searching** and **fearless moral inventory** of **ourselves.**

5. **Admitted to God,** to **ourselves** and to **another human being** the exact nature of our wrongs.

6. Were **entirely ready** to **have God remove** all these **defects** of character.

7. **Humbly asked** Him to **remove** our shortcomings.

8. Made a **list of all persons we had harmed,** and **became willing** to **make amends** to them all.

9. **Made direct amends** to such people **wherever possible,** except when to do so would injure them or others.

10. **Continued** to take **personal inventory,** and when we were wrong **promptly admitted** it.

11. **Sought through prayer** and **meditation** to **improve** our **conscious contact** with God, as we understood Him**, praying** only

for knowledge of **His will for us** and the **power to carry that out.**

12. Having had a **spiritual awakening** as the result of these steps, we **tried to carry** this **message** to alcoholics, and to **practice** these **principles** in **all our affairs.**

[My bolded type]

HUMILITY

The Course addresses the central Twelve Step concept of humility (reflected throughout the Steps and cited specifically in Step Seven) in several places in all three of its volumes. As an example, in the Text it says, "...the essential thing is learning that *you do not know*. Knowledge is power, and all power is of God. You who have tried to keep power for yourself have 'lost' it. You still have the power, but have interposed so much between it and your awareness of it that you cannot use it. Everything that you have taught yourself" [i.e., through your ego] "has made your power more and more obscure to you" (296T, 1:1-5).

Eastern spiritual approaches such as Buddhism have addressed humility in their concept and practice of "don't know." I define humility as being open to learning about self, others and God. Both a Twelve Step approach and the Course see our attachment to our ego as our major stumbling block to true knowledge and peace. The ego thinks it knows it all, which is a key problem if we attach ourselves to it (wrong mind). Pain is our usual result. The Course offers a way out of this unnecessary pain. It says, "Your part is very simple. You need only recognize that everything you learned you do not want. Ask to be taught, and do not use your experiences to confirm what you have learned. When your peace is threatened or disturbed in any way, say to yourself:

'I do not know what anything, including this, means. And so I do not know how to respond to it. And I will not use my own past learning as the light to guide me now.'"

By this refusal to attempt to teach yourself what you do not know, the Guide Whom God has given you will speak to you. He will take His rightful place in your awareness the instant you abandon it, and offer it to Him." (297T, 6:3-11). What it is suggesting here is the miracle, or the whole loving and usually ultimately peaceful experience of choosing God/Holy Spirit/Christ over the ego.

I describe and discuss more similarities between the Twelve Steps and the Course in the companion volume to this one called *Teachers of God*.

5 Relationship to the Bible

The Course does not invalidate the message of the Bible. Rather, it views the Bible's words as being valid starting points and supports most of them, while offering some new interpretations and understandings. While the Course agrees with most of the Bible and treats it with an attitude of respect, it also clarifies some of its misunderstandings (Watson 1997).

In his book *Seeing the Bible Differently:* How ACIM views the Bible (1997), ordained minister Allen Watson speaks from his experience of studying the Bible in depth for 22 years, while searching for its promises of peace and understanding. Ultimately he became frustrated and discouraged, gave up the Bible, and continued his search elsewhere. Several years later he found the Course and has studied it just as seriously for the past 11+ years. During this time he found four ways that the Course relates to the Bible with their: 1) Similarity, 2) Continuity, 3) Difference, and what he and his colleague Robert Perry call 4) "Qualified supersession" (i.e., reinterpretation). I will touch on each of these now and refer the reader to Watson's book for more examples and discussion.

Similarity

Some examples of the many similarities in both books are shown in Table 1. In each of these the Course respectfully refers to one or more of the Bible's references and then gently comments on them. Regarding the *Holy Spirit* and that *God is Love* the Course fully agrees, and then greatly expands into a description of them, giving more details and principles. On *Christ* and the *crucifixion* and *resurrection* the Course has much to say in continuity and notes some differences, and offers a few reinterpretations (qualified supersessions), as shown in the Table 1 **Similarities Between the Bible and ACIM,** and in Tables 2 and 3 following.

Concept	**Bible Ref.**	**Total Number**	**Course Ref.**	**Total Number**
God is Love	1 Jn 4:8 & 4:16	2	eg 162T, 9:7;608T,8:7	14+
Holy Spirit	Jn 14:16-17	33	eg 75T,2:5; 89M,1:1	758
Christ	Heb 2:10	Numerous	eg 87M,2:1	**many**
Crucifixion	1 Pet 2:24	many	eg 94T,12:1	
Resurrection	Dan 12:1-3; I Cor 15:3-7	0	eg 94T,12:1	
Forgiveness	Acts 2:38; Heb 10:2	several	eg 252T,1:1	**numerous**
Oneness & Unity	De 6:4; Acts 17:16-28	few	eg 101T, 6:12	
Peace	Ps 119:165; Isa 32:17	250+	eg 129T, 10:8	

Table 1.

Similarities Between the Bible & ACIM

The Hebrew Bible (Old Testament) *alludes* to *forgiveness,* while the New Testament *names* it as a way of experiencing peace. The Course then *builds on* it and *describes* it, as I outline throughout this book and especially in its last three chapters. Regarding *oneness* and *unity,* and *peace,* the Course relates these to the Bible and builds on them similarly.

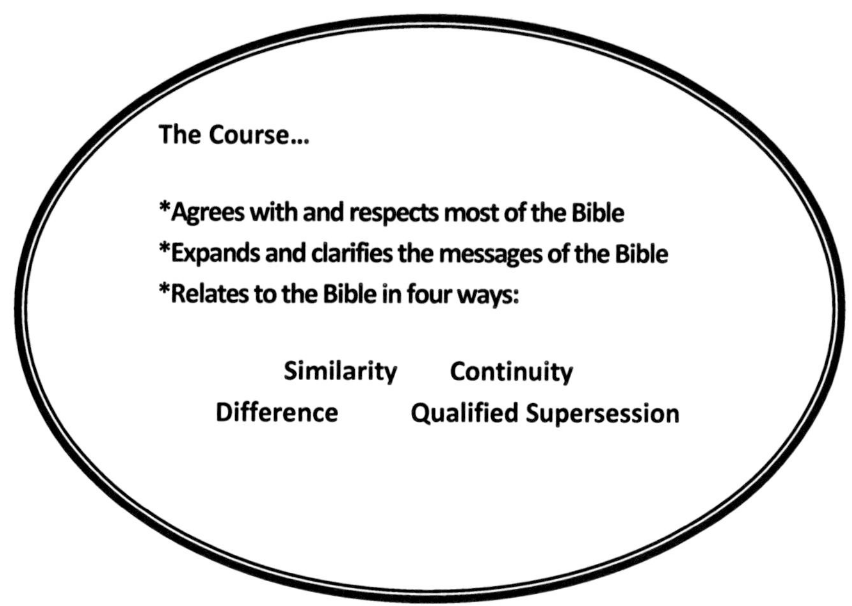

The Course...
*Agrees with and respects most of the Bible
*Expands and clarifies the messages of the Bible
*Relates to the Bible in four ways:
Similarity
Continuity
Difference
Qualified Supersession

Continuity

There are numerous spiritual topics in both the Old and New Testament on which the Course discusses and elaborates. It thus *continues* the divinely inspired dialogues and teaching of the Bible, thereby addressing them in *continuity* in more detail. Table 2 gives four clear examples, which show a remarkable expansion and evolution of our spiritual development over time that are clarified by the Course.

Difference

There are some important and spiritually useful differences between the Course and the Bible that are beyond simple continuity, which I describe throughout this "Bird's eye View." Some are also addressed in Tables 1 and 2 above, and other examples are in Table 3 in the next chapter.

Hebrew Bible/ Old Testament	*New Testament*	*ACIM*
Need to overcome self-centeredness	**Jesus models** and **teaches transcending (ego)** self	Specific **ways to let go of ego** eg 104-111T
Love our neighbors	**Love** & **pray for** our **enemies** Lk 10:25-37	We have **no enemy** eg 563T,3:6
To handle guilt from our sins: **1) animal sacrifice,** **2) day of atonement,** **3) obey God's laws**	**Faith in Jesus**	We have **no sin or guilt** eg 556T, 10:5
Kingdom of God = Israel; political	Kingdom = **at hand; *in* us**	Kingdom = ***is* us** eg 60T; I:3-5

Table 2.

Examples of Continuity among the Hebrew Bible, New Testament and A Course in Miracles

(Compiled and expanded from Watson 1997)

QUALIFIED SUPERSESSION

While acknowledging the truth of the Bible, the Course goes deeper into that truth. Here, it explains some misunderstandings that some of the human and therefore, at times, likely naturally ego-involved writers of the Bible may have presented. Watson (1997) says, "The relationship of the Course to the Bible is much more like an amendment to the Constitution than it is like one law that completely replaces another. The kernel of the old meaning still stands, but now has been amended -- clarified, explained differently, corrected in certain aspects, enhanced and refined to a higher level."

If we re-examine Table 2 above, we can see that in these four examples there is not only similarity and continuity from one book to another, but there are also gradual differences. Some of these differences include how the Course re-interprets them by a process which Watson and his colleague Robert Perry call qualified supersession (p 23 above)..

These observations of continuity and qualified supersession are found in at least 20 more concepts that both the Bible and the Course address. While discussing each of these in detail is beyond the scope of this "Bird's Eye View," I list and briefly describe these in Table 3 in the next chapter.

THE QUESTION OF AUTHORITY

But how can we know or prove that the Course has an equal or perhaps even a greater authority than the Bible? The answer may depend on the religious beliefs of the individual reader/observer and their life experience when using any of the material. To most Jewish clergy and people the New Testament is heretical and has no religious or spiritual value to them. Although the Course has now (in 2010) been published for 34 years, most Christian clergy and people are unaware of its existence or have only heard of it in passing. Many who have heard of it appear to reject it without studying it, especially fundamentalists, who view it as being heretical. The Course says that it is but one of many approaches to God. Its tone is gentle, like one of the characteristics of a teacher of God (12M, 1&2), and the Course does not try to force itself on any reader.

I agree with Allen Watson that there is no easy way to prove that the Course has greater authority then the Bible. He says, "...I had enough openness of mind to overlook, for the time being, the troubling way the Course attempted to correct the Bible, which in my opinion was arrogance. I read it anyhow for the things I could agree with, the things I found helpful. Those fragments of Course teaching turned out to be more effective in bringing me peace of mind and happiness than the entire Bible had ever been. I saw miracles happening in my life, and in the lives of those around me. Those experiences with the Course opened my mind to question my fundamental assumptions about the Bible's complete reliability." Numerous other ordained ministers such as Jon Mundy, Tony Ponticello, and Paul Phelps also teach the Course.

The only "proof" of any holy book is what happens in the life of each of its students. Does it work for them? Do their relationships with self, others and God improve? The Course says, "This course offers a very direct and a very simple learning situation, and provides the Guide Who tells you what to do. If you do it, you will see that it works. Its results are more convincing than its words. They will convince you that the words are true." (173T,9:1-4) This reminds me of the saying, "It works!" from Twelve Step Programs.

*   *   *

I have not seen any arrogance in the Course. I have sometimes felt overwhelmed when reading it for very long. That is why I like to read it in short amounts of a page or two at a time. Over the past 33 years I have found the Course to be helpful in making my relationships work better with myself, others and God.

Since 1983, I have taught some of the principles of the Course as a part of the many workshops I have given nationally on spirituality. For 3 years I taught a class that focused specifically on the Course, with my wife Barbara Whitfield, to a total of about 100 people at the Rutgers University Advanced School of Alcohol and Drug Studies. Most of these students considered themselves to be seeking spiritual nourishment and, after studying the Course, many said they were beginning to experience some positive changes in their lives.

Based on the sales of the Course and the early commentaries on it, nearly 2 million people own a copy or have read it and/or are studying it. Watson said, "Thus, in my opinion, the best way to see the relationship between the Course and the Bible is to understand the Course as the next major step in revelation after the Bible. It is *grounded in the Bible*, it *takes up* the *truths* the Bible was trying to impart to us, but it *presents them in a higher form*. Some have said the Course might be thought of as 'The Third Testament' and that is, in my mind, a title the Course merits, although I believe the Course can stand by itself, apart from the Bible, much more easily than the New Testament could stand apart from the Old." [my italics] (Watson 1997)

PHOTO OF THE ORIGINAL TYPED COURSE MANUSCRIPTS IN BOUND FORM

6 The Kingdom Within: an Experience of Peace

The Course says that a part of God, the Holy Spirit (God's Loving and healing Energy), and Christ are within each of us. While it uses Christian terminology, it transcends some conventional Christian beliefs and expands them (Table 3 - which shows still more examples of how the Course expands some of the Bible's messages.). By doing so, it demystifies, clarifies, and makes many of the conventional understandings more practical and useful. It is thus a more universal spirituality that respectfully rises above and transcends many traditional religious faiths, while at the same time enfolding, supporting, and nurturing them.

In addition to having ***in*** each of us a part of God, Holy Spirit and Christ, associated with these we also have as a direct result the Kingdom of Heaven in each of us. As shown in Table 3, rather than experiencing the Kingdom only when we die, in Heaven, we actually have it now, in what the Course calls the *Holy Instant*. In Chapter 4, "The Illusions of the Ego", it says:

"It is hard to understand what 'The Kingdom of Heaven is within you' really means. This is because it is not understandable to the ego, which interprets it as if something outside is inside, and this does not mean anything. The word 'within' is unnecessary. The Kingdom of Heaven is you. What else but you did the Creator create, and what else but you is His Kingdom? This is the whole message of the Atonement; a message which in its totality transcends the sum of its parts. You, too have a Kingdom that your spirit created. It has not ceased to create because of the ego's illusions. Your creations are no more fatherless than you are. Your ego and your spirit will never be co-creators, but your spirit and your Creator will always be. Be confident that your creations are as safe

as you are. The Kingdom is perfectly united and perfectly protected, and the ego will not prevail against it. ..." *(*60T,1:1-13)

It can be described as though one minute we are standing, experientially, in our ordinary reality and life, in our ordinary feeling state of discomfort or tension, but at the same time we begin to look through a veil at Heaven, or peace, which is located on the other side of the veil. **If we step through the veil** into Heaven, we feel peace, facilitated by God's unconditional Love, which is the Holy Spirit. We are now not just *in* the Kingdom, but as we experience it, we *are* the Kingdom.

We may reach such an experience of peace through prayer, meditation, or while having a peak experience (as Abraham Maslow, Walter Pahnke, B. Whitfield and others have described.) Once in the Kingdom, the Holy Instant, we can now turn and look back through the veil, and see and experience, as we step back through the veil into our previously "ordinary" experience that *it also* can be and *is* the Kingdom. Now on both sides of the "veil," the peace of God exists for us to experience within our consciousness, and our heart.

The author of the Course, Jesus the living Christ, says, "When I said, 'My peace I give unto you,' I meant it. Peace comes from God through me to you." (185T,6:6-7) "Only at the altar of God will you find peace." (187T,11:1) We can experience the Kingdom, the Holy Instant, God's peace, when a miracle happens - when we choose God over the ego.

In the long Table 3 on the next page, I show 21 more examples of conventional Christian ideas as they are expanded in *A Course In Miracles.* I will be referring to some of these throughout this book and in my second volume *Teachers of God*, which I wrote as a companion book to *Choosing God*.

Table 3.

Examples of Conventional Christian Ideas as Expanded in ACIM

Example	*Conventional Christianity*	*Expanded in ACIM*
Miracle	Observable or tangible event	Choosing God over ego; a shift in perception
Christmas	Celebrates Jesus' birth	Celebrates birth of holiness (308T)
Apostle Judas	Betrayed Jesus by turning him over to the Romans	Jesus did not believe in betrayal or condemnation, & thus did not judge Judas (95T)
Easter	Focuses on crucifixion & resurrection	Focuses on resurrection (94;425T)
Peace & Joy	In Heaven	Can have it now (308-9T)
Littleness & Judgment v. Grandiosity	Emphasizes self-deprecation & avoiding grandiosity	Encourages magnitude & grandeur (305T)

Table 3 (Cont'd) ***Example***	***Conventional Christianity***	***Expanded in ACIM***
Magnitude, Grandeur & Greatness	Discourages	Describes it in each of us (306-9T)
Kingdom of Heaven	In Heaven, only when we die	We have it now in Holy Instant (309T)
Love	Vague; agape	Core of our being (308-9T)
Part of God	Jesus in our heart	In us, creatures, & all living things
Word of God	Logos; Jesus (Jn1:1)	God's answer correcting belief in separation; Holy Spirit, Atonement,
Christ	Only one Christ, as Jesus	As Christ in each of us, ultimately as the Sonship
First Coming	Jesus as the only Son of God	Jesus was created, like us, as the Son (Child) of God (pp 64, 170T)

Table 3 (Cont'd) ***Example***	***Conventional Christianity***	***Expanded in ACIM***
Second Coming	Fear, judgment, threat (ego's plan); a dramatic physical and spiritual event (Mt. 24:26-31)	End of ego's rule & healing of the mind; Holy Spirit's correction of ego's plan; the undoing of what never was; spiritual experience of awakening from the dream (170T)
Earthly Life	Sin, guilt & shame	Ego's dream; a learning experience
Sin - Many references are in Course	We are inherently bad and separated from others and God	Correctable mistakes return to sanity (the sense that we are innocent and separation never happened)
Judgment	Judgment as attack & punishment	God does not judge; our pain is unnecessary
Devil	Fallen angel, Satan	Ego gone awry

Table 3 (Cont'd) ***Example***	***Conventional Christianity***	***Expanded in ACIM***
Hell	Place of eternal pain	Living in ego's world (301-3T)
Atonement	Paying for our sins & reconciling with God	Separation never happened; ego's world is not real; judgment & attack are not justified
God's Will	Vague	Complete peace & joy; Co-creation with God (182W)

7 Levels of Understanding

Some Course readers have told me how at times it was difficult for them to understand what it says. When I first started reading it in 1977, I became confused and eventually lost interest in it for nearly a year. I had jumped into it too fast, and at the same time it was starting to overwhelm my ego. When I returned to it later at a more leisurely pace, I felt better about it and gradually began to understand it more.

One possible reason for misunderstanding it is what the Course calls *levels* of understanding, about which we may experience *level confusion* (e.g., 23T,2:2-3; 24T,1:6; and 26T,5:2-6) As Ken Wapnick (1985) describes it, level **two** is the easier to understand, where it addresses our **personal psycho-spiritual experiences** in our body in this world. In various ways it addresses our attachments, addictions and compulsions, wherein we may think that we can't be fulfilled or happy unless we have another's body, money, food, drug, car, job, power or lifestyle, all of which are aspects of special relationships. Christ awoke from this unhappy dream (i.e., his experience of level two) before we did. He realized, among other things, that our attackers are not actually attacking us, but are calling for help. He did so by changing his perception, by using his right mind.

We can use our level two experiences to learn to shift our perception to that of level **one**, which is what the miracle helps us learn. Level one is harder to understand and experience. It sees our **life from a higher level**, through the **eyes of Christ**, as described in the Course. Here truth is only of Spirit, in God and God's world. The Holy Spirit uses our level two experiences, if we choose to let It help us, to teach us about the reality of living in level one. We can summarize these two levels as being a paradox, about which we can use the miracle to begin to understand, as shown in Table 4. If this seems complicated, it often is in early reads.

Bear with me.

Table 4.

The Paradox of the Journey Home:

Some Characteristics of Two Levels of Understanding in ACIM

Level	*Characteristics*	*References*	*Responsibility*
1 **Creation** **"macro"**	**God & God's world** **One-mindedness** **The Trinity; Peace**	**Home** **Knowledge** **Holy Instant**	**God does**
↑	***Practice miracles* by *choosing God***		↑
2 **"micro"**	**The struggle in choosing God's world over ego's**	**The Journey Home**	**We do our part, then turn it over**

Describing these two levels further, Wapnick says, "The Course... is written on two levels, reflecting two basic divisions. The first level presents the difference between the One Mind and the split mind, while the second contrasts wrong- and right-mindedness. On this first level [1/one], for example, the world and body are illusions made by the ego, and thus symbolize the separation. The second level [2/two] relates to this world where we believe we are. Here, the world and the body are neutral and can serve one of two purposes. To the wrong-minded ego they are instruments to reinforce separation and to the right mind they are the Holy Spirit's teaching devices through which we learn His lessons of forgiveness. On this level, illusions refer to the misperceptions of the ego: e.g., seeing attack instead of a call for love, sin instead of error." (Wapnick 1989)

On the next page is a chart from Wapnick's 1990 book *A Vast Illusion*: Time according to *ACIM* that further helps illustrate his above statement.

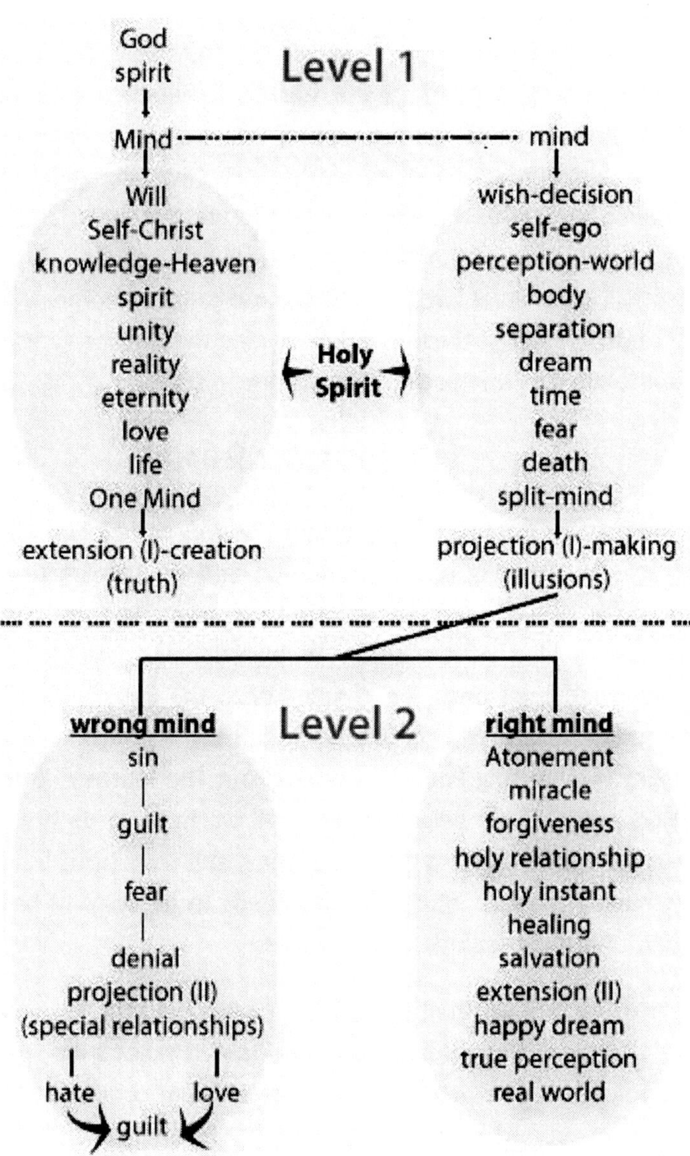

Chart 1.

Levels Clarification in ACIM

(used by permission from Wapnick 1990)

Level one thus represents God and God's world and aspects of the "separation" and "duality," bridged by the Holy Spirit. Level two represents several aspects of our earthly experience that we have to negotiate *and* which can at the same time *assist* us in negotiating them. These include our ego and its world, including sin, guilt/shame, fear, projection and special relationships. While we can try to understand the Course's description of the dynamics in level one, most of our work in this lifetime will be in level two, as we take our journey Home. With the two of Its "feet" in each of these two levels, plus the division in level one, the Holy Spirit helps us bridge the "gap" between them.

THE JOURNEY HOME

In his booklet on the Course called *The Journey Home*, Allen Watson (1994) uses a clarifying chart wherein he outlines the Starting Point and The Journey, which correspond to level two, and the Goal of the Curriculum (a kind of transition to experiencing level one), and the Ultimate Goal, level one (see chart). With the *assistance* of God/Holy Spirit/Christ, we are responsible for exploring and attaining all of level two, from The Starting Point and throughout The Journey. But after that, God/Holy Spirit/Christ does the rest. All we have to do are any bits or parts of the various phases on our journey, and then turn the rest over to God, who will then do whatever else needs to be done to help us reach the goals of the curriculum.

As in using any spiritual path, what I have learned from studying the Course and practicing its suggestions is that it takes time, patience and some dedication. The psychospiritual growth that comes is usually similar to the "educational" variety discussed at the end of the "Big Book" of Alcoholics Anonymous, wherein our growth or progress comes slowly, in fits and starts.

CHART OF THE JOURNEY HOME

Starting Point		The Journey				Goal of the Curriculum		Ultimate Goal
	The Turning Point	Phase One: Escaping From Darkness		Phase Two: Emerging Into Light			God's Last Step	
Wrong-Mindedness		Step One: Beginning Thought Reversal	Step Two: Preferring the New Thoughts	Step Three: Beginnings of Extension	Step Four: Vigilance for God and His Kingdom	Right-mindedness		One-mindedness
The World False Perception Nightmare		Conflicting thought systems Fear as ego is uncovered Learning I cannot be attacked by anything external	Diminishing conflict Increasing willingness to see my ego as the problem Learning my attacks on others are unjustified	Determination to end conflict Decision to hear only Holy Spirit Joining with companions on the journey	Vigilant against conflict Watchful for unrecognized ego thoughts Extending forgiveness to my brothers and the world True Perception	Real World True Perception Happy Dream		Heaven Knowledge Awakening

Chart 2.

Chart of The Journey Home
(from Allen Watson 1994, used by permission)

As mentioned above, I see our journey as a part of the Divine Mystery that we are each exploring in our own way and in our own time. For me, the Course has been the single most helpful guide to exploring and living the Mystery that I have found. In one of its most often-quoted lines the Course describes the other side of the paradox of the "journey."

It says,

"The journey to God is merely the reawakening of the knowledge of where you are always, and what you are forever. It is a journey without distance to a goal that has never changed" (150T,9:6-7).

Seek not to change the world, but choose to change your mind about the world.

A Course in Miracles, p 415 T

---

8 STAGES OF RECOVERY AND HEALING

There may be many reasons why someone doesn't understand the Course, which I said above. In addition to being 1) a simple mismatch, where the person may have no interest in it, or there being 2) too much conflict generated when the person compares it to their religion of origin or practice, there is also a difficulty that may be related to 3) the stage of recovery or healing that they are in when they read or study the Course.

For years I have divided the stages of recovery into three. In Stage • **Zero**, the person has an active illness or disorder which may be acute, recurring, or chronic, and they have not yet started in recovery for it (see Table 5). Unless they heal or recover from it, it is likely that the disorder will distract them from the ability to focus fully on Stage Two or Three recovery work or on the Course.

At Stage • **One**, recovery begins. It involves participating in a full or partial recovery program to assist in healing the Stage Zero condition or disorder.

Stage • **Two** involves healing past wounds from childhood or other trauma, and this may take several years to heal in a full or partial recovery program (Table 5).

Stage • **Three** involves spirituality and its incorporation into daily life, which the Course addresses so well.

This Stage-oriented developmental sequence is an ongoing process for most of us, as shown in Table 5 on the next page.

Recovery Stage	Condition	Focus of Recovery	Approximate Duration	Understanding and Using ACIM
3	Human/ Spiritual	Spirituality	Ongoing	**Easier**
2	Past Trauma	Trauma-Specific Recovery Program	3-5+ years	**Some Difficulty**
1	Stage 0 Disorder	Basic Illness Full Recovery Program	½ to 3 years	**Difficult**
0	Active Illness	Usually None	Indefinite	**Most Difficult**

Table 5.

Recovery and Duration According to Stages
With Ease of Understanding ACIM

While the Course may be useful in any of these stages, it may be more *difficult to understand* in Stages Zero, One and Two and then easier to understand and use at the end of Stage Two and throughout Stage Three recovery. One reason for this progression is the difficulty we may have with a number of core psychological and spiritual issues when we are *distracted* by having a Stage Zero disorder or illness, combined with the fact that we still *may not experientially know* our *Real Self*. (Whitfield 1987, 1991, 1993).

When a person tries to jump from Stage Zero or One to Stage Three, without doing recovery work in Stage One and/or Two, it is as though they are --consciously or unconsciously-- trying to bypass these intermediate stages. Some have called this a "spiritual bypass," or trying to know God before we know our Real Self.

For these and other reasons, I do not recommend that a person read the Course in any depth much before they reach the last phase of Stage Two recovery. One important part of Stage Two work is giving an accurate name to a lot of things, such as the components of our inner life, core recovery issues, and past traumas. Only when we accurately name these and grieve them can we most successfully let go of them. It is this process of letting go where the Course can be so helpful.

BILL AT THE TYPEWRITER

9 WHO IS THE COURSE ABOUT?

So far I have discussed some of *what* the Course is about. In the following chapters I will give an overview of *who* it is about, i.e., its main characters, actors or beings. At its highest level it is about One Person. It is about God. The two major parts of God that the Course describes in some detail are the Holy Spirit, which is God's unconditionally loving Divine Energy, and the Child (my gender-equal term), which it calls the Son (the individual person) and the Sonship (the collective of all of us).

The Child or each of *us* individually, has the ability, awareness or consciousness at all times to choose, by free will, to be in conscious or unconscious contact with God -- or *not*-with-God, which is usually the ego.

THE EGO

The ego is a "player" that is actually neither a player nor a person. It is a temporary and illusory kind of assistant or entity that the Course says that we made, and which God did not make. Why would we make the ego? The Course doesn't give a clear answer. My personal guess is that we made the ego to help us sort and navigate as we journey on this divinely mysterious adventure of our life on this planet.

The Course talks a lot about the ego. It mentions or describes many of its characteristics, which I list in Table 6. As I read over these characteristics, I see few, if any, desirable ones. They are all mostly undesirable, and it is painful to be in the line-of-fire when the ego commits nearly any of these crazy (and crazy-making) thoughts and behaviors.

About the only ones that I can see in Table 6 that can be occasionally useful are *some* of the *painful feelings*, which can help us with grieving and setting healthy boundaries, as I describe below. It can also be useful at rare times to be *dishonest* with unsafe others, such as if we were to be taken captive by a terrorist. And vigilance is useful in most circumstances, but I think what the Course means here is that the ego is *vigilant* for separation and negativity, and not for God and God's kingdom.

DEFINING EGO

But my above opinions aside, the Course describes essentially no constructive uses for the ego. Like a helicopter that flies over and over in different circles above and around a building to photograph it from many different angles and views, throughout its three volumes the Course circles the ego and describes its characteristics and "dynamics" from many different perspectives. One of the first indirect references to the ego comes in Chapter 2 of the Text, where it refers to the ego's four distorted beliefs.

These distorted beliefs include that:

1. **What God created can be changed by your own mind** (see Table 6. Characteristics of the ego from ACIM, below),
2. **What is perfect can be rendered imperfect or lacking,**
3. **You can distort the creations of God,** and
4. **You can create yourself, and that the direction of your own creation is up to you.**

It says, "These related distortions represent a picture of what actually occurred in the separation, or the 'detour into fear.' None of this existed before the separation, nor does it actually exist now." (17T, 1:9-12 & 2: 1-2)

Table 6.

Characteristics of the ego from ACIM

(see e.g., Findisen 1983 p 101-125; Wapnick 1997; & ACIM)

Belief or idea	**Dissolves Joy**	**Peace is its Greatest Enemy**	**Uncreative**
Separation	**Divisive**	**Poor Decision or Choice**	**Unpredictable**
Scarcity	**Defensive**	**Projects to Deceive**	**Unstable**
Fear, guilt, shame, anger, confusion (and generates them)	**Defends that Sin is Real**	**Exclude and Destroy**	**Untrusting**
Blocks Communication	**Dishonest**	**Promotes Special Relationships**	**Vicious**
Body is it's Symbol	**Does Not and Cannot Love**	**Preoccupied With Unsolvable Problems**	**Wrong Voice**
Capriciousness	**Fragments**	**Speaks First and Loudest**	**Analyzes**
Compares	**Fears Death, Yet Wants You Dead**	**Seeks Love, Yet Distorts it and Does Not Find It**	**Conditional**

Table 6.

Characteristics of the ego from ACIM

(Continued)

Complex	Grandiose	Accepts What	Holy Spirit Rejects
Condemns	Ignorant, Unknowing	Suspicious	Cunning and Baffling
Conflicted	Illusion, Not Real	Savage	
Confuses, -ing	Insane	Symbol of Separation	
Denies Free Will	Incapable of Knowing Our Feelings	Sacrifices	
Deprives	Judgmental	Takes Others' Inventory	
Desperate	Lives in Time	Tormenting	
Devil	Littleness (promotes)	Traitor	
Dispiriting		Teaches that Sin and Error Are Real	
Distracting	Made by Us, Not By God	Part of Mind That Believes In Separation	

The ego is mentioned directly in Chapter 3, "The ego is the wrong-minded attempt to perceive yourself as you wish to be, rather than as you are. Yet you can know yourself only as you are, because that is all you can be sure of." As I have referred to it in *Healing the Child Within*, the ego is the false self, and by contrast "...as you are," and "...all you can be sure of" is the True or Real Self, which can also be called the Soul or Human Heart, as it is connected to God, and which the Course calls right mind.

It continues, "The ego is the questioning aspect of the post-separation self [us after we thought we left God], which was made rather than created. It is capable of asking questions but not of perceiving meaningful answers, because these would involve knowledge and cannot be perceived." (42T, 2:3-4).

IDENTIFYING THE EGO

One way to suspect that we are in our ego is if we are experiencing *tension, fear, conflict, anger, guilt* or *shame*, and at that moment, we have not chosen God. In short, if we don't feel peace, we are likely to be in or attached to our ego.

Based on my own life experience and the experience that I have gained from assisting many people as they heal from hurts, losses and traumas, there is a potentially difficult block to our being at peace for very long even if we do choose God over our ego. In the active process of **grieving** that hurt, loss or trauma, we may be in our True Self, and not in our ego. The problem is that the genesis of these same painful feelings has double-edged sword qualities, in that they may be from authentic grief *or* from ego attachment. The figure on the next page may help clarify this idea.

Since we can experience any and all of these painful feelings when we are grieving, it can take some practice to learn to differentiate that healthy grief from being in our ego. In healthy grieving, we often feel a bittersweet sadness and we usually feel a *movement* or *flow* in our grief, i.e., we don't feel stuck (which others and I equate with "depression").

The Course teaches us that no matter where we are on this spectrum, we can choose God. But the ego is cunning and baffling. It will continue to

Figure 1.

Spectrum of Feelings from ego-Attachment to Grieving to Choosing God

ego Attachment	…………	***Gray Zone of Grieving***	……………	***Choosing God***
Fear, Shame Tense	**Anger, Guilt, Conflicted**	**Grief, Confused**	**Contentment, Compassion**	**Peace, Love**

try to convince us that it can offer us something and that it will always act on our behalf. The Course suggests that we not believe such seduction and empty promises, on which the ego is incapable of delivering.

Examples of the Course's concentrated discussion and description of the ego are in the Text on pages 65 through 69 and 202 through 207, and at the end of the Manual for Teachers (in the *Clarification of Terms* section, pages 81-2). Regarding the "dynamics" of the ego, on page 203 of the Text it says, "'Dynamics' implies the power to do something, and the whole separation fallacy lies in the belief that the ego *has* the power to do anything... . Yet the truth is very simple: *All power is of God. What is not of Him has no power to do anything.* ...The ego's goal is quite explicitly... ego autonomy. From the beginning, then, its purpose is to be separate, sufficient unto itself and independent of any power except its own." (203T,3:3-7; 4:4-5). This is in large part why, when we let our ego run our life, we tend not to do as well in our relationships, emotions, and well-being.

*   *   *

The above are a few examples of what the Course says about the ego, which *we made* and is *not real*. Yet thinking that we needed it to survive, and being taught by some of our earthly authority figures to identify with it and use it, we took it on as though it were our identity. But at every moment in our life the Course offers us this one simple idea and choice: whenever we are in pain, we can choose God over our ego.

The ego lives by comparisons.

The ego cannot survive without judgment.

A Course in Miracles, pp 52 & 54

BILL AND HELEN

10 God

The Course's introduction says, "Nothing real can be threatened. Nothing unreal exists. Herein lies the peace of God." God and God's world, which includes each of us and our experience of the Divine Mystery, is real. It is invulnerable and safe, so we might as well relax and enjoy our part in it.

The Course says that God is our most important relationship. It says, "For God created the only relationship that has meaning, and that is His relationship with you." (322T, 6:6) This is another view of the notion that it is all God. Everything. Everything that is real is God and part of God's world.

What Is God Like?

But how can we even begin to describe such a mysterious Entity or Being that is so great that It involves everything that is real? My answer and that of many others (e.g., Perry 1993, 2008) is that we can't. So, what follows are but some brief words about That which cannot be described in words, which is one of the characteristics of God: ineffability.

The Old Testament says that God said, "I am that I am" (Ex 3:14), and the Course says " 'God is,' and then we cease to speak, for in that knowledge words are meaningless. There are no lips to speak them, and no part of the mind sufficiently distinct to feel that it is now aware of something not itself. It has united with its Source. And like its Source Itself, it merely is." (323W, 5: 4-7)

In reviewing the Course and an early *Concordance* to the Text (Findisen 1983), I found over 30 characteristics of God described in the Course that we can consider (Table 7). I've noticed that there are no threatening, judging, scary or other negative characteristics of God anywhere in it.

In fact, the Course says clearly that God is ***not***:

1) **Vengeful** (the Course says, " ...'vengeance is mine' *means* to give your vengeance to God, who will outshine it and undo it in you by dissolving it" (87T, 7:1-3) 2) **Jealous** (*we* are jealous, not God, it says), 3) **Punishing**, or 4) **Judging**, in contrast to some interpretations from the Bible by some of its authors or readers. According to the Course, God clearly does not will that we suffer in any way.

As Robert Perry (1993), a longtime student and writer on the Course says, "If you could take the positive notions of God that you have inherited from Western spirituality--of a God that is loving, merciful, wise, just -- and then elevate, expand and purify those concepts to the highest possible degree, and send them out into infinity, far, far beyond where your limited mind can go, you would have some distant notion of the God of the Course."

Is ("I AM")	Infinite	Formless
Source, Creator, Causal	Eternal	In Us
Father (beyond gender)	One	Quiet
Real, Reality	The Universe	Undefended
Peace, Joy, Heaven	Creative	Unconflicted
Home (i.e., our real Home)	Unconditional Love	Asks devotion
Ineffable (Divine Mystery)	Unchangeable	Safe
Limitless, Omnipresent	Power	Paradoxical
Matrix, Container	Knowledge	Trusts us perfectly

Table 7.

Some Characteristics of God from ACIM

What does God give each of us?

Two of God's characteristics stand out throughout the Course: **creative** and **unconditional love** ("God is love" 1Jn 4:8 & 16) so that we can say that in part, God is creative unconditional Love. While we don't know exactly how God is so creative, the Course says that God creates by *extending* or giving that Love.

Just what does God give to each of us? The Course says that God gives us *everything, all there is,* which includes His love and light, meaning and mercy, and that we both *have* the power and *are* the power to create for ourself, which He also gives us. Finally, God gives us His Will and *Himself,* which means that we are God's extension, i.e., God is *in* each of us.

From reading the Course for over 30 years, I've progressively gotten the sense that God has poured a *lot* of Himself, a *lot* of Godliness, into each of us. And it says that a way to begin to realize that fact is to practice choosing God over our ego at any time that we are in pain, conflicted, tense, angry, resentful, or upset.

The Course says that we are God's only creation: "God created nothing besides you and nothing beside you exists, for you are part of Him." (181T,2:1) Then it introduces another paradox: *"Your creations add to Him as you do, but nothing is added that is different because everything has always been."* 181T,2:4) How can God and God's world be at the same time changeless *and* extending and creating? This idea is so uncomfortable to our rational mind that we have to use words like paradox to describe it. Yet in God, as part of the Divine Mystery, the Course says that this seeming paradox is all at peace.

God's Will for Us

God has also given us His Will. The Course tells us a lot about exactly what God's Will for us *is.* God wills that we each not be bound by any negativity, such as pain, suffering, "sin," or death. Indeed, God wills that we have perfect happiness now, that we create with Him and that we share His Love and light.

God's Will for Us:
*No Pain
*Peace and Joy Now
*Co-Create with God

Finally, God's will is *us*, which the Course calls the Son or the Sonship (the sum of all of God's creation), of which we are each a necessary and crucial part. Indeed, it says that without us God is lonely, and that we are also lonely without God. It says, "God and His creations are completely dependent on Each Other. He gave them His peace so they could not be shaken and could not be deceived. ... God is lonely without His Sons, and they are lonely without Him." (22T, 5:6-8,11) If we were to take these words literally, we might surmise that God is also a *feeling* Being, who feels Love, loneliness for us at times, and occasionally even weeps for us (89T, 4:5). In this regard, we might ask, are feelings *human* characteristics or *Godly* ones? Perhaps they are both. By contrast, Ken Wapnick views the Course's statements such as these as being metaphors or symbols, to go beyond their literal meaning to their true meaning.

What God creates is eternal (74T,5:6), and since God created us, we are eternal. We have nothing to fear from God, and since the ego is not real, we don't need to fear it either. So, most of our fear is unnecessary. We can relax. This is one of the benefits of reading the Course and practicing its principles, since reading it can help us experience peace. I've noticed that on the days that I read it and/or meditate, I feel better. I feel less fear, tension or conflict. For me, that's "good medicine"-- it works, *and* it's free and non-toxic.

In the next volume *Teachers of God* I devote an entire chapter to describe still more of what the Course says about God's Will for us (Chapter 10, on pages 67 through 71).

"God and His creations are completely dependent on Each Other. He gave them His peace so they could not be shaken and could not be deceived. ... God is lonely without His Sons, and they are lonely without Him."

A Course in Miracles, pp 22T,5:6-8, 11

---

11 The Holy Spirit

The Holy Spirit is the bridge from God and God's world to this world as we know it. Often, God can seem so abstract and vast that we may have difficulty connecting, reacting, and realizing God, but the Holy Spirit can and does assist us in our having these joyful experiences. The ways that It does that are many, which I summarize in Table 8 on the next page.

The Holy Spirit is basically an extension *and* an extender of God and God's Love to and for each of us. It is the intense and never-ending unconditional love by which God somehow carries out the Divine Mystery of creation and existence. But this Love that we call the Holy Spirit is so intelligent and gentle that it knows exactly how to assist us with what is best for our own individual needs. To get that help, all we need do is ask, which is what happens any time that we choose God over the ego.

The Course says that the Holy Spirit is our healer, comforter and guide, our perfect teacher. God created It when the separation, which has also been called "the Fall," seemed to occur. In that unholy instant when we thought we separated from God, we felt a sudden rush of fear, guilt and shame, and we have not stopped feeling these since. We felt and still feel these painful feelings because we still think that we've left God, that we are somehow bad for doing so, and that God will therefore punish us.

But the Course says that God created the Holy Spirit at the same instant that we first thought that we separated from God. So anytime that we feel separated or feel any of these painful feelings or any other pain, we can ask any member of the Trinity for help, and we will be thereby choosing God over our ego.

The following table highlights some of the characteristics of the Holy Spirit, as described in ACIM.

Healer	Universal or Shared Inspiration	Mediator Between Spirit and ego
Comforter	Spirit of Joy	Way Atonement Heals
Guide in Choosing	Calls for God and Return To Joy	Radiance and Glory
Perfect Teacher	Mind for God	Quiet
The Answer to The Separation and Everything	Idea and Thought of God	Our Communication with God
Motivation for Miracles and Miracle Mindedness	Reminds us of Home In God	Choice for God Great Correction Principle
In Each of Us (In Our Right Mind)	Voice for God and God's Will	Brings God's Love
Close to Knowledge	Voice for Creation	Strengthens the Kingdom Within
Incapable of Attack, Controlling and Arrogance...Merely Reminds	Translates: • Communication into Being •Perception into Knowledge	Leads us to God

Table 8.

Characteristics of the Holy Spirit from ACIM

Our Connection and the Dual Function

Countless references to the Holy Spirit are spread throughout the Course. I will mention two of the more concise ones here. The first and simpler one is from the end of the Manual for Teachers, where it addresses how *connected* we are to the Holy Spirit. It says that Jesus and *each of us* are the *manifestation* of the Holy Spirit. It says that, "He [the Holy Spirit] has established Jesus as the leader in carrying out His plan since he was the first to complete his own part perfectly." (89M,2:2)

Wapnick (1984) describes the "bridge" function of the Holy Spirit by the metaphor of It having both of its "feet" in two worlds: God's and ours. This notion is described in what the Course calls the dual function of the Holy Spirit, where it says, "He knows because he is part of God; He perceives because He was sent to save humanity. He is the great correction principle; the bringer of true perception, the inherent power of the vision of Christ.... He never forgets you. And He brings the Love of your Father to you in an eternal shining that will never be obliterated because God has put it there." (89T,3:3-9)

The Undoing Process

My second selected reference to the Holy Spirit is more complex and in my experience usually takes a while to practice and achieve. It is about what the Course calls the *undoing process*, i.e., the undoing or letting go of the ego. While this process is described in different ways throughout the Course, it does so in its most concentrated form in the section called "The Lessons of the Holy Spirit" on pages 103-111 in Chapter 6 of the Text. Here it summarizes this process in three statements: 1) To have, give all to all. 2) To have peace, teach peace to learn it. And 3) Be vigilant only for God and His Kingdom. I have meditated on these sayings countless times over the years and read this section many times over, and I'm still not completely sure of exactly what the term "all" means. In statement number one my current sense is that *all* here means peace, love and acceptance, which was the message of the New Testament, although the Course greatly clarifies these three terms throughout its pages.

Steps	***Comments Summarized*** from ACIM
To have, give, all to all	Preliminary. We turn in that direction and thereby take charge. May appear to bring conflict. Holy Spirit is with us in each of these steps. (106T,6:1-9)
To have peace, teach peace, to learn it	We have and are what we teach or project, and strengthen it by what we believe and think. Conflict (from ego) continues and then gradually lessens. While still preliminary and perceptual, affirms that we want peace and is a step to peace. To desire wholly is to create. The Holy Spirit will lead us on. (106-108T)
Be vigilant only for God and His Kingdom	Teaches us not to judge, transforming projection into extension. We eventually learn that vigilance is not necessary for truth, and everything outside of the Kingdom is illusion. (108-111T)

Table 9.
Outline of the Undoing - *of the ego* – Process

This section describes how, while initially difficult, these three steps are progressively easier to achieve as we follow them along, and which I summarize in Table 9. After looking over this outline, you may want to consider studying Chapter 6 of the Text, and then sitting back and observing what comes up for you in your inner life. When I have done that, I've noticed a conflict, in that I had an approach-avoidance experience with it. I felt some peace as I contemplated this approach, and was thereby compelled to continue studying it, while at the same time I often felt uneasy. But the more that I've read and studied it, the more I've been able to let go of my ego and feel God's love and peace, which has then lessened the tension that I've felt in some difficult situations and relationships.

For me, all of the above has taken a long time to assimilate, and it has sometimes been difficult. Because of this, and knowing what I do about the Course overall, I do not recommend that anyone who is new to the Course try to delve into this section on the undoing process right away. Rather, a more gentle approach might be to read the Course slowly over time, in small bits, to gradually digest its message. Then without rushing, read Chapter 6 when you get to it.

The Holy Spirit in Other Faiths

The Course uses the traditional Christian term of Holy Spirit. Other faiths call It by different names. Buddhists and Taoists have called It *Chi* or *Ki* energy, and Hindus have referred to It in part as *Kundalini* energy. Jews call It *Ruach Ha Kodosh* and Native Americans have called It *Spirit.* But these all appear to be the same loving, healing and creative Energy of God, which is also inside of each of us.

When we choose God over the ego, we can spiritually "reach out" to any member of the Trinity -- to God, to the Holy Spirit, or to the Christ, since these are each parts of the Totality of God.

Give faith to one another, for faith and hope and mercy are yours to give.

A Course in Miracles p 394 T

---

12 Who Is The Christ?

The *New Testament* was apparently inspired by God and Jesus, but Bible scholars over the last century, including those in *The Jesus Seminars* (Funk et al 1999), say that it was written by mostly unknown followers of Jesus. What is remarkable about the Course is that it was written in its entirety by the living Christ. To many of us, short of God, it would be hard to have come from a much higher authority.

Conventional Christianity acknowledges but one Christ, as the historical and still living Jesus. The Course expands this understanding as the Christ that lives in and as each of us:

"There must be doubt before there can be conflict. And every doubt must be about yourself. Christ has no doubt, and from His certainty His quiet comes. He will exchange His certainty for all your doubts, if you agree that He is one with you, and that this Oneness is endless, timeless, and within your grasp because your hands are His. He is within you, yet He walks beside you and before, leading the way that He must go to find Himself complete. His quietness becomes your certainty. And where is doubt when certainty has come?" (511T, 9:1-7)

While it makes similar identifications of Christ within us throughout, the Course becomes perhaps the clearest toward the end of the Manual for Teachers:

• "There is no need for help to enter Heaven for you have never left. But there is need for help beyond yourself as you are circumscribed by false beliefs of your Identity, which God alone established in reality." (87M, 1:1-2).

• "...The name of *Jesus* is the name of one who was a man but saw the face of Christ in all his brothers and remembered God. So he became identified with *Christ*, a man no longer, but at one with God." (87M, 2:1-2).

• "... Is he the Christ? O yes, along with you. His little life on earth was not enough to teach the mighty lesson that he learned for all of you. He will remain with you to lead you from the hell you made to God. And when you join your will with his, your sight will be his vision, for the eyes of Christ are shared. Walking with him is just as natural as walking with a brother whom you knew since you were born, for such indeed he is." (87 & 88 M, 5:1-6).

THE FIRST AND SECOND COMINGS

What are the first and second comings of Christ? Convention says that the first coming is the life of the historical Jesus as the only son of God. It also says that the second coming will be a physical and spiritual event that, according to Matthew, appears to be threatening (24M: 26-31).

As introduced in Chapter 5, the Course comments and sometimes expands upon the Old (Hebrew Bible) and the New Testament in several ways. These include: 1) by *reinterpreting* the Bible, thereby providing a clearer understanding of the intent of what was said (or actually said), and/or 2) by writing a *separate* and *different explanation of what was intended* by God, a Prophet, or Jesus. In the following, it uses both of these kinds of expansion:

"The First Coming of Christ is merely another name for the creation, for Christ is the Son of God. The Second Coming of Christ means nothing more than the end of the ego's rule and the healing of the mind. I [Jesus] was created like you in the First, and I have called you to join with me in the Second. I am in charge of the Second Coming, and my judgment, which is used only for protection, cannot be wrong because it never attacks. Yours may be so distorted that you believe I was mistaken in choosing you. I assure you this is a mistake of your ego. Do not mistake it for humility. Your ego is trying to convince you that it is real and I am not, because if I am real, I am no more real than you are. That knowledge, and I assure you that it *is* knowledge, means that Christ has come into your mind and healed it." (64T, 10:1-9).

A key here is "I was created like you in the First, and I have called you to join me in the Second." This statement and others in the Course imply that Christ was and is our older brother, and is not different from us except that he woke up sooner than we did and has developed his awareness of his spirituality beyond where we have. His experience and evolution have given him the wisdom and knowledge to write the Course for us. He says that since he is our Teacher and older brother we should respect him, but not be in awe of him. Awe should be reserved for God. (16T, 5:1-11)

***First* Coming** **God created Jesus and all of us, i.e., the Sonship.**
***Second* Coming** **End of the ego's rule and the healing of the mind.**

Seeing Christ in Others

How difficult is it for us to see the face of Christ in others? Does it take practice? The Course says that the Christ in each of us is not found in our body: "The Christ in you inhabits not a body. Yet He is in you. And thus it must be that you are not within a body." (518T,1:1-2) It also says: "...See your brother as yourself. Framed in his body you will see your sinfulness, wherein you stand condemned. Set in his holiness, the Christ in him reclaims Himself as you. (519T, 2:7-9). And: "No one who carries Christ in him can fail to recognize him everywhere." (518T, 2:1).

It seems to take time for us to see Christ in others and in ourself. Studying the Course can help us in this regard, as it assists us in choosing God and thereby practicing miracles and forgiveness/letting go of ego.

*   *   *

In the next chapter we will also see that the Christ is even more: God's one Son as unified mind and spirit. The Christ is also our spirit, soul, and true Self-- all of these terms being synonymous with one another. How does the Course define and describe these and other related terms, which are parts of each of us? I will outline these in Chapter 13.

13 The Mind

"...mind is...the activating agent of spirit." (79C,1:1)

I have written some books about the healing process from a developmental perspective that also have a strong base in self psychology and object relations theory and practice[3]. In each of these I speak from various perspectives about a central theme: the True or Real Self that gets so overwhelmed, wounded and traumatized in this troubled world and in its own dysfunctional family so often that to survive, it "goes into hiding" deep within the unconscious part of its own psyche. At that point, to run the person's life, a false self emerges and tries to take over, although it eventually fails. Another name for this false self is the ego. Wapnick (1991) said, "The word 'ego' is used in the Course to denote the false self that was made in opposition to, and as a substitute for the Self of Christ that God created and which is our true spiritual Identity."

In contrast to the few useful qualities of the ego, such as being our assistant or sidekick at times, as described by Lazaris in 1986, the Course appropriately addresses only the negative aspects of the ego, since that is what blocks our ability to know and experience God and God's world, Love and peace.

In my understanding of the True Self, which I also call the Child Within, and the terminology of the Course, the True Self can be equated with the

---

[3] These books include ***Healing the Child Within, A Gift to Myself, Co-dependence: Healing the Human Condition, Boundaries and Relationships, Memory and Abuse, The Truth about Depression,*** and ***The Truth about Mental Illness.***

mind as it experientially connects with God through the spirit that is inherent within itself, and which the Course calls ***right-mind.*** In Table 10, I clarify some of the similarities among these two terms True Self and false self from self psychology and approximately equivalent terms used in the Course.

Self Psychology	*Approximate Terms used in the Course*		*Also Within Ourself*
True self	**Right Mind** ↕ **Miracle**	**Mind (active; chooses God)** **spirit (real; soul; creative)** **consciousness (receptive)**	**God** **Holy Spirit** **Christ**
false self	**Wrong mind**	**Mind chooses ego and/or doesn't choose God**	**ego ("devil")**

Table 10.

Similarities among Terms in Self Psychology and ACIM

THE MIND AND OUR INNER LIFE

A major and basic part of our True Self is its rich *inner life*, which the Course touches upon as it describes various aspects of the mind. Some of these aspects of the mind include: *consciousness, spirit, experience, decision, choice, learning, communication,* and *freedom* -- to name a few. Throughout its three volumes, the Course discusses different facets of each of these. As a start, to better understand these terms I have found that the section "Clarification of Terms" on pages 77 through 92 at the end of the Manual for Teachers to be helpful. Here it defines some of these terms in a more linear way that we can begin to explore. For example, in defining the mind, it says:

"The term *mind* is used to represent the activating agent of spirit, supplying its creative energy. When the term is capitalized it refers to God or Christ (i.e., the Mind of God or the Mind of Christ). *Spirit* is the Thought of God which He created like Himself. The unified spirit is God's one Son, or Christ. " (79C,1:1-4)

"In this world, because the mind is split, the Sons of God appear to be separate. Nor do their minds seem to be joined. In this illusory state, the concept of an 'individual mind' seems to be meaningful. It is therefore described in the course *as if* it has two parts; spirit and ego."(79C, 2:1-4)

Some aspects of the mind	• **Consciousness** • **Spirit** • **Decision /Choice maker**	• **Learning** • **Communication** • **Freedom**

SPIRIT

Table 10 (above) and its three following paragraphs give us an introduction to how central our mind is as we experience life from day to day, since a major part of our mind is *spirit*. God's Spirit is in each of us. The Course goes on to say that our spirit is always connected to and in contact with God "...through the Holy Spirit, Who also abides in this part [i.e., spirit] but sees the other part [i.e., other components of the mind] as well. The term 'soul' is not used except in direct biblical quotations because of its controversial nature. It would, however, be an equivalent of 'spirit,' with the understanding that being of God, it is eternal and was never born." (79C,3:1-3) I will describe spirit further in the next chapter.

RIGHT AND WRONG MIND

As I mentioned in previous chapters, our mind is a double-edged sword. It can go with God or the ego, and can thereby be right or wrong. The Course says,

"*Right-mindedness* listens to the Holy Spirit, forgives the world, and through Christ's vision sees the real world in its place. This is the final vision, the last perception, the condition in which God takes the final step Himself. Here time and illusions end together."

"*Wrong-mindedness* listens to the ego and makes illusions; perceiving sin and justifying anger and seeing guilt, disease and death as real. Both this world and the real world are illusions because right-mindedness merely overlooks, or forgives, what never happened. Therefore it is not the *One-mindedness* of the Christ mind, Whose Will is one with God's."(79M, 6:1-3)

In Tables 11 and 12, I list several characteristics of these two kinds of mind from the Course. The mind is the crucial part of us where we initiate choice and behavior. I see the Course as a sophisticated and potentially effective intellectual and experiential training process for our mind.

By reading and studying it, we can each learn to differentiate and initiate miracles, forgiveness and God's Love and peace instead of the painful fear, guilt and shame of the ego's illusory world.

CONSCIOUSNESS

The Clarification of Terms section of the Course describes a final part or aspect of the mind: *consciousness*. It says that consciousness is the *receptive* mechanism, receiving messages from the Holy Spirit *or* the ego. It continues, "Consciousness has levels and awareness can shift quite dramatically, but it cannot transcend the perceptual realm [discussed below]. At its highest, it becomes aware of the real world, and can be trained to do so increasingly." (80C,7:4-5)

Table 11.

Some Characteristics of Right Mind from ACIM

(continued top of next page)

The activating agent of spirit (the part of the mind in contact with God through Holy Spirit)	**Creative & powerful when links with God.**
Links us with God.	**Communicates. Contains loving thoughts.**
Can learn, by which we can change.	**Means by which we determine our own condition.**
The mechanism of decision; can value & decide what to give and receive.	**Wills to know (it's proper function.)**
Free. Creates reality when accepts the Atonement.	**When serves spirit, is invulnerable and can't be defiled.**
Healed, it radiates health & healing.	**Can heal the body.**

Can experience the pure joy of revelation.	**The innocent mind has everything, cannot project, & strives only to protect its integration and wholeness.**
Restored to fullness by miracles.	**Never sleeps.**
Is real. Soul.	**When quiet, it remembers God.**
Peace	**With our brothers and sisters, we each dwell in the Mind of God.**

While consciousness does not initiate miracles (which unite us directly with ourself, others and God) or revelation (which unites us directly with God), these crucial relationships are *experienced* in consciousness. Consciousness may also induce action, but it does not inspire it. (7T, 1:1-8) Christ inspires miracles (5T, 32:1) and the Holy Spirit brings and inspires revelation, (8t, 5:1-5) which is an intensely personal, experiential, union and conscious contact with God (7T, 2:1-7).

In Chapter 3 of the Text the Course says, "Consciousness, the level of perception, was the first split introduced into the mind after the separation, making the mind a perceiver rather than a creator. ...The ego is a wrong-minded attempt to perceive yourself as you wish to be, rather than as you are. Yet you can know yourself only as you are, because that is all you can be sure of. Everything else *is* open to question." (42T, 2:1&3-5)

Table 12, on the next page, lists some characteristics of what the Course calls Wrong Mind.

Identifies with ego, body, or separation	**Feels pain, especially fear, guilt and shame.** * * * ***Comments follow***
When does so, can deceive itself and err, thus making up illusions by believing in them	**None of our mind's errors mean anything, since they don't exist**
Confused	**Holy Spirit lets our mind re-interpret its misperceptions**
Determines its perceptions and projects them	**We can learn to change our mind about our mind**
Projects own conflict and pain, but by doing so won't lose them	**We always have the power to change our mind**

Table 12.

Some Characteristics of Wrong Mind

from ACIM

God is the light in which I see.

God is the mind in which I think.

God is the love in which I forgive.

God does not forgive, because He has never condemned.

A Course in Miracles, p 98-99 T

---

14 In The Spirit

The Course says, "...to be *inspired* is to be in the *spirit*." When we choose God over our ego we immediately become *right-minded, inspirited*, and feel *peace*. We feel more real. The resulting miracle is also the experience of our self-starting this process. We start it by choosing God. All that follows then is a continuation and reverberation of the *miracle*. The miracle continues as a catalyst (5T,37:2) or trigger to opening our mind to God through our mind's chief component called spirit, which I conceptualize as part of the "big cosmic picture," and which is actually happening in the inner life of each of us from moment to moment, as shown in Figure 2 on the next page. This figure shows a proposed graphic illustration of the interrelationship among some of the key terms in the Course that it describes and discusses throughout its pages. However, this scheme is but a map, and the map is not the territory. At the same time, maps can be useful.

The figure shows God and some major components of God's world, according to my understanding of the Course. God created what the author of the Course calls the *Sonship* (i.e., the son/daughtership) which constitutes all of us children of God. In this diagram the circles represent two of God's individual children in relationship with each other and God. Through God's unconditionally loving, healing and creative Energy, the Holy Spirit, as we live in this world we are able to experientially communicate with God, a process that Twelve Step fellowship programs call "conscious contact."

Spirit ...Continued from Chapter 13

Each of us is a unique and crucial child (and thus a part) of God. The Course says, "You are altogether irreplaceable in the Mind of God. No one else can fill your part in it, and while you leave your part of it empty your eternal place merely waits for your return." (179T,10:1-2) As a child of God we each have a mind which is powerful and creative and which has two parts: spirit and consciousness (Figure 2 below). Our spirit, which the Course also calls our Self, is an *extension of God and God's Holy Spirit*, through which it is in complete and direct communication with God, as shown below in Table 13 on page 84. It can thereby *co-create* with God through prayer, meditation and God-contemplation at any and all times now.

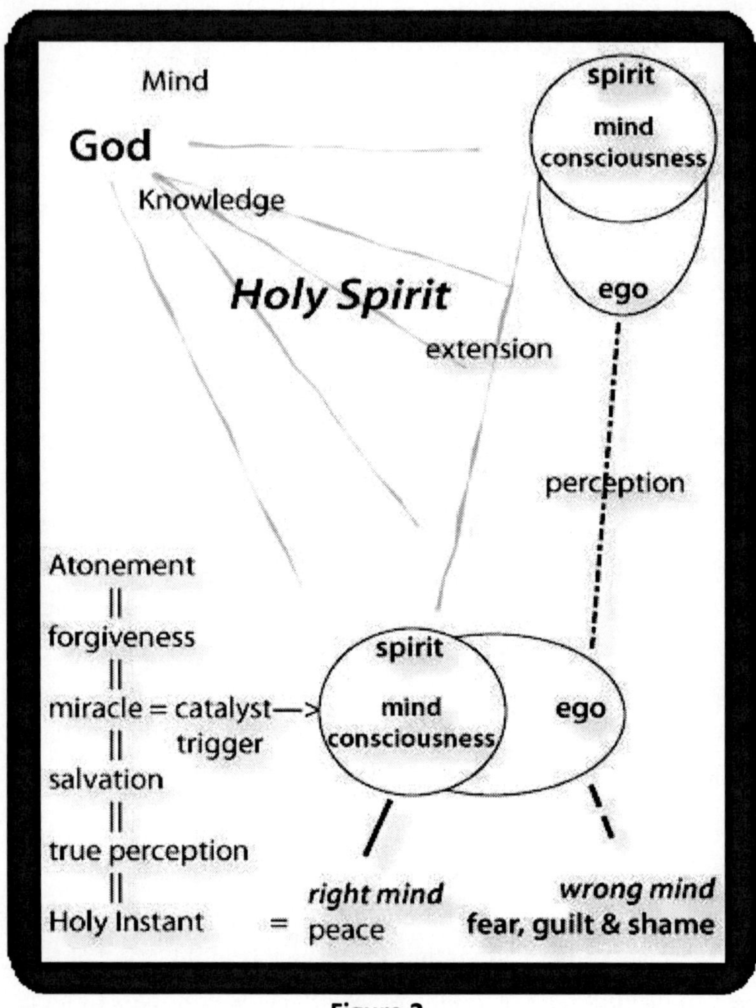

Figure 2.

A Scheme of the Interrelationship among Some Terms in ACIM

The Course says that our spirit is neither conflicted nor attacking, and is incapable of knowing or projecting darkness of any kind. Sharing and giving, it wills to extend God's Being, which is its only function. It knows God completely and shines in God's Mind. Our spirit is a major part of each of us, and it cannot perceive falsely and does not need to learn. Because it is unchangeable, unshakable, perfect, immortal, and eternally free, our spirit is *invulnerable.*

We Forgive for What Did not Happen

"Invulnerable" means that it (our core, or mind-spirit-consciousness, which some call Real/True Self and I also call Child Within) is not capable of being hurt or harmed *long term*. This spiritual fact is why we can, if we choose, let go of or forgive any hurt or wrong that we may have experienced or perceived. This is because no matter what anyone does *to* us or does *not* do *for* us, we are *not harmed* at our core in a lasting way. As part of his teaching, Christ showed us this fact as his resurrection. In the section on "The Message of the Crucifixion" in Chapter 6 of the Course, he says:

- "I elected, for your sake and mine, to demonstrate that the most outrageous assault, as judged by the ego, does not matter. As the world judges these things, but not as God knows them, I was betrayed, abandoned, beaten, torn, and finally killed. It was clear that this was only because of the projection of others onto me, since I had not harmed anyone and healed many." (93T,9:1-3)

- "You are not persecuted, nor was I. You are not asked to repeat my experiences because the Holy Spirit, Whom we share, makes this unnecessary." (94T,11:1-2)

- "The crucifixion cannot be shared because it is the symbol of projection, but the resurrection is the symbol of sharing because the reawakening of every Son of God is necessary to enable the Sonship to know Wholeness. Only this is knowledge." (94T, 12:1&2).

The crucifixion was an extreme example that Christ, who lived here as Jesus of Nazareth, used to teach us that *we too are invulnerable*, and thus we need not fear any harm from anyone or any thing. Nor, at a lesser extreme, when a person expresses anger at us or when we get angry at anyone (perhaps from our ego's false perception), and build up a resentment, do we need to carry the toxicity of that anger and resentment around inside us to our own detriment. At either of these points of upset -- fear or anger, or any other upset -- we can chose God, which results in letting go of our attachment to it, or forgiveness, and which is also the miracle, salvation, true perception, *and* the Atonement. The resulting peace that we feel will also reflect that we are now in the Holy Instant, as shown in the left lower section of Figure 2 on page 82 above.

Never conflicted or attacking and **incapable of darkness**
Sharing and **giving**
Co-creative with God
Wills to **extend God's Being**, which is its only function
In complete and direct **communication with God** and creation
Knows God completely
Cannot perceive and does not need to learn
Shines in God's Mind
Unchangeable, unshakable, perfect, immortal, and **eternally free**

Table 13.

Some Characteristics of spirit

from ACIM

At the same time, the miracle is a catalyst that triggers (Figure 2 above) our experience of our True Self as mind-spirit-consciousness that is inspirited by experientially remembering its inherent connection to God. So our mind, which is our decision- and choice-maker, by choosing God, Holy Spirit, or Christ, sets the positive cycle of experience in motion: in-spirit → miracle → in-spirit. By choosing God over our ego, God's Holy Spirit gently guides us back to what I call our Real Self or Child Within (what the Course calls child of God, which *is* our mind-spirit-consciousness).

CONSCIOUSNESS ...CONTINUED FROM CHAPTER 12

Our *consciousness* is what the Course calls the more receptive part of our mind. It can receive either God's unconditional love or the ego's confusion and pain. Our mind is the active part of us that chooses God or not. When we are *not* at peace, that decision and choice for God is made by our mind, which is how our mind is so powerful and creative. By choosing God, our mind thus activates the miracle and the miracle then opens us to experiencing our spirit and God.

The blameless cannot blame, and those who have accepted their innocence see nothing to forgive. Forgiveness is the means by which I will recognize my innocence. It is the reflection of God's love on earth.

A Course in Miracles, p 99 T

---

15 Perception and Knowledge

The miracle is the same as a number of other terms that the Course uses, including forgiveness, salvation, and true perception, as shown in Figure 2 in the previous chapter. (85M,3:6) Ordinary or false perception is what we do through our ego, and perception is not Knowledge. We see, hear, sense, analyze and understand others and the world through our ordinary perception (or ego), which is not Knowledge or Truth, and we thereby miss what we could see through Christ's vision, which the Course also calls *true* perception. I list other terms for these two opposing kinds of perception in Table 14 on the next page.

Perception

Perception results from ego attachment (an ancient Buddhist observation) and projection. *What we think is wrong, conflicted, or missing* from inside us *we project onto others* (people, places and things -- in Twelve Step wisdom) outside of us. *What we project we then see and hear,* which is our ordinary perception, which the Course calls *false perception*. It uses similar terms as well, including distorted, meaningless or wrong perception. All of this kind of perception is related to our individual consciousness (as shown in Figure 2 in the previous chapter). The Course says: "Consciousness, the level of perception, was the first split introduced into the mind after the separation, making the mind a perceiver rather than a creator. Consciousness is correctly identified as the domain of the ego". (42T, 2:1-2)

But when we do not choose God or when we choose ego, we cannot see and hear, i.e., perceive accurately, through this usually dysfunctional aspect of our mind, which the Course also calls wrong mind. The way that we can see and hear the most accurately for now is through our *right mind*, when we *choose God*, and which is *true perception*. This correct kind is also called right, sane, perfect, or redeemed perception, which the

Course calls *innocence* (to which the romantic poets such as William Blake often referred), the *happy dream*, and *Christ's vision*. True perception is guided by the Holy Spirit, and while it is still a form of perception, it is our path to the One-mindedness of God and Christ which the Course says belongs to God's Knowledge.

Perception	***Equivalent***	***Mechanism***	***Other Descriptors***
false	**wrong mind**	**from ego and projection; makes fear**	**Distorted, meaningless, wrong, selective, misperception**
True	**Right Mind**	**Guided by Holy Spirit, Path to Knowledge and joy**	**Correct, accurate, perfect. Right, sane, redeemed, happy dream, innocence, Christ's vision**
none needed	**One Mind (God's Mind)**	**Knowledge God's last step "I need do nothing"**	**Reality, God and God's World, One-mindedness, Heaven, Awakening**

Table 14.

Terms for True and False Perception as Contrasted to God's One Mind

ONE MIND

To reach and realize the Mind of God and Christ is *not our job*. All we need to do is to accept the Atonement for ourself, which we achieve by accepting the unreality of sin, guilt/shame and death, and instead, experiencing miracles, which come when we choose God. Then God will take us the rest of the way to God and God's Mind, which is God's last step.

God's Mind is among the most abstract and least discussed terms in the Course, although it does discuss God's Mind far more than the Bible does. From his understanding of the Course, Wapnick (1989) describes One-mindedness as, "the Mind of God or Christ; the extension of God which is the unified Mind of the Sonship transcending both right- and wrong-mindedness; One Mindedness exists only at the level of knowledge. The One mindedness of [God and] Christ is the world of Heaven or knowledge: the pre-separation world of spirit, love, truth, eternity, infinity, and reality, where the oneness of God's creation- the sum of all His Thoughts- is unbroken. It is the natural state of direct communication with God and his creation that existed before the mind of God's Son thought of separation. In this state the perfect unity of the Trinity is maintained."

ACCEPTING THE ATONEMENT …OUR ONLY TASK

- ***Realize* the *unreality* of sin, guilt/shame, & death**
- ***Experience miracles***

KNOWLEDGE

What is the knowledge of God? In Table 15 I list some terms that the Course uses to describe it, and contrast these with some of the terms that it uses to describe perception. From his long study of the Course Wapnick (1989) describes knowledge as, "Heaven, or the pre-separation world of God and His unified creation in which there are no differences or forms, and thus it is exclusive of the world of perception." The Course's use of the term transcends our conventional use of the term knowledge by reflecting "pure experience with no subject-object dichotomy."

Knowledge	**perception**	**Knowledge**	**perception**
Truth	Illusion	Unconditional	Selective
Peace in God	Body, sin, guilt, fear	Understandable	Confusing
Law of Love/ God	Law of ego/world	Factual	Interpretive
Unalterable	Alterable	Stable	Unstable
Eternal	Transient	Reality	Dream
Unambiguous	Ambiguous	Peace	Conflict
No beginning/ end	Beginnings & endings	Unity/ Atonement	Belief in opposites
Timeless/ spaceless	Space & time	Holy Relationship	Special relationship
Given	Learned	Abundance	Scarcity

Table 15.

Some Characteristics of the Worlds of Knowledge and perception in ACIM

God's Knowledge is thus pure experiential knowing. In our current experience as humans, one of the closest experiences to this kind of knowing might include a *natural knowing* of God that transcends belief, faith, righteousness or the like. When the spiritually oriented psychiatrist Carl Jung was asked in a BBC interview whether he *believed* in God, Jung paused for a few seconds and then answered in a now famous response, "No. No. I know [God]."

Being on different levels, these two domains -- knowledge and perception -- cannot meet. Only one correction of perception is possible: *true* perception, which is the same as forgiveness (letting go and letting God), miracles, salvation and Atonement. All of these are healing and transient aids to assist us on our journey Home.

The best way that I know to learn more about all of these terms and their descriptions is to read and study the Course and practice its principles, the most basic of which is that whenever we are in any kind of pain, we can choose God.

What is healing but the removal of all that stands in the way of knowledge.

A Course in Miracles p 188T

---

16 SEEING THE WORLD DIFFERENTLY: EXTENSION OR PROJECTION?

Extension of God's Love is fundamental, unchangeable and continues forever.

The beginning of Chapter 21 of the Text says these now classic words, "Projection makes perception. The world you see is what you gave it, nothing more than that. ...It is the witness to your state of mind, the outside picture of an inward condition. ... Therefore, seek not to change the world, but choose to change your mind about the world." (455T,1:1-2,5,7)

PROJECTION MAKES PERCEPTION

As I mentioned in previous chapters (2, 9, 11, and 15), the Course says that we each thought that we separated from God, which the Bible metaphorically called "the fall." We then believed in that notion of separation, and we felt pain in our experience of guilt and shame (that we were bad for leaving God), mixed with fear (that God would punish us for being bad). The ego, which represents the separation in our minds, told us that *it* could save us. First, it said that we should *deny* feeling the guilt/shame and fear, and if that doesn't work, to *dump* (project) that pain onto others, which the Course calls one kind of special relationship.

The Course describes these two defenses against pain -- denial and projection -- as unhealthy devices that the ego conceives and institutes regularly in our daily lives. In projecting what is inside of us onto the world as special relationships we then try to give our pain to people, places and things. We see *them* as guilty and shameful, and blame them for our unhappiness by attacking them, as we project our anger onto them for causing our pain. Chapter 6 of the Text says, "Projection means anger, anger fosters assault, and assault promotes fear." (92T, 3:3)

We thought that others were out to get us and were even crucifying us. By doing so we see or perceive a dark world, and all of our seeing and perceiving are happening unconsciously.

EXTENSION CREATES PEACE AND LOVE

We can thus understand how projection makes perception, and thereby re-enforces the separation that we thought we experienced from others and God. But we have another choice. Each time that we choose God over the ego and its projection/perception, we metaphorically "see" more clearly, i.e., with true perception, which will then allow us to remain open to the Holy Spirit's extension of God's love that constantly radiates from God --and from us, because we are a part of God. The crucifixion is the symbol of projection, but the resurrection, our own awakening to the experience of God and God's world, is the symbol of sharing (as shown in Table 16), which is also part of extension.

Term	*Symbol of*	*Term*	*Symbol of*
Crucifixion	**Projection**	**Real World**	**End of unhappy dream**
Resurrection	**Sharing**	**Atonement**	**Seeing the face of Christ**
ego	**separation**	**Christ**	**End of guilt and shame**
body	**ego**	(see also pp iv, 40, 51, 52, 83)	

Table 16.
Some Terms Associated with Symbols in ACIM

While the ego made projection, God gave us the ability to extend, and what we project or extend is real for us (114T,2:4). What we project we believe (114T,3:1), but what we extend is real and is what we are as well (3:6), i.e., a child of God. Extension is fundamental and. forever. It is similar to the inner radiance that God gave each of us (17T, 2:4).

The first paragraph of Chapter 2 of the Text says, "To extend is a fundamental aspect of God which He gave to His Son. In the creation, God extended Himself to His creations and imbued them with the same loving Will to create. You have not only been fully created, but have also been created perfect. There is no emptiness in you. Because of your likeness to your Creator you are creative. No child of God can lose this ability because it is inherent in what he is, but he can use it inappropriately by projecting."

We create, or actually *co*-create, by extending our unconditional love each time that we choose God and experience the peace of a miracle. We extend when we are in our right mind, when we reflect God's inner radiance of love through the Holy Spirit that is within and outside of us, as shown in Table 17 on the next page. When we extend God's love to others, ourself, and back to God, we and others feel better physically, mentally, emotionally and spiritually. We all can thereby feel peace and grow psychospritually. Could this experience be related to the serenity about which A.A. and the other Twelve Step fellowships speak in their sharing when we so extend love to another?

Why would we get back, through our perception, what we give out through projection? While I don't know the answer, I wonder if the answer could be that this is God's way of helping us to bring our pain into the Light of God, which can eventually "heal" us by outshining it. I put "heal" in quotes because according to the Course we are already perfect just as we are.

When we project, a major result is that we end up attacking ourself, since we magnify our pain by projecting it onto the "screen" of others, where we then see and hear it more acutely. By doing that, we suffer, since we take it back in by believing that it is real, and the upset and unnecessary pain that we feel usually ends up hurting us. What we thus give and believe, we get.

Characteristic	*Projection*	*Extension*
Mechanism	ego's failed attempt to get rid of guilt/shame and fear	God's inner radiance of Love through Holy Spirit
Mind	Wrong mind	Right Mind
Conscious	No	Yes
Promotes	Separation (false perception)	Unity (true perception)
Associated Feelings	Guilt/shame, anger, fear	Love and peace
Result	We and others feel worse	We and others feel better
Reality	Unreal, illusion	Real

Table 17.

Characteristics of Projection & Extension In ACIM

Two Levels of Extension

The Course addresses two levels of extension. *Level two* extension is related to true perception. Here our and God's extension works by "extending the Holy Spirit or Christ's vision in the form of forgiveness or peace;" Extension is "the Holy Spirit's use of the law of mind, contrasted with the ego's projection." Wapnick (1989) Based on my understanding of the Course, this is the kind of extension that I have described above.

But there is another kind of extension, one that is possibly even more a part of the Divine Mystery. Perhaps it is even a crucial part. This kind is related to God's Knowledge and is therefore associated with *level one* extension. Here extension involves "the ongoing process of creation, wherein spirit flows from itself." But to discuss this in much detail is not the purpose of the Course, and this level of extension is not our job anyway -- it is God's. Our only job is to accept the Atonement for ourself, which we eventually do when we practice miracle-mindedness, each time that we choose God.

Let forgiveness be the substitute for fear. This is the only rule for happy dreams.

A Course in Miracles p 590T

---

17 FORGIVENESS

For me, forgiveness has been the most difficult idea to understand in the Course. This is in part because it is discussed in such a circular manner throughout its three volumes that it is hard to find a section that defines it clearly and comprehensively. Like many of its readers, I've had to dig it out by reading, re-reading and then focusing on any sections where it is mentioned more than just in passing.

In my understanding, the Course does **not** address or use the term forgiveness to mean **absolving others of their responsibility** for their actions and inactions or **not protecting us from trauma**. Rather, it describes forgiveness as a level 2 function that helps us know our self, others and God better, as shown in Table 18 on the next page. The forgiven world thus becomes our self-created gate into Heaven, where we can finally forgive ourselves and remember God, who then takes the final step in our return to Him.

WHY FORGIVE?

If we are each already perfect and not a sinner, as the Course says, then why would we need to forgive or be forgiven? While there may be many answers to this question, the Course says that each time that we forgive (which is true perception and the experience of a miracle), we heal our pain (fear, guilt and shame) from our imagined separation from others and God. It says that God appointed our self-inflicted attack and wounds to be a means of transforming their curse (i.e., pain and suffering) into the gift of our salvation and peace. (530T,6:6) In the forgiveness process, when we ask for help, it is the Holy Spirit that then does the transforming.

But in my experience we usually have to know at least two things before we can ask for help with any specific conflict or pain.

First, as I have described in most of my other writings, it helps to know cognitively and experientially the *nature* of the curse (the conflict or pain), including its *name* (e.g., the accurate name of a hurt or trauma experienced) and its associated pain. Stage Two recovery work will usually help us with this task (outlined in Table 5 on page 46). Gloria Wapnick (1997) summarized this principle clearly: "You have to do the hard work first, and then you ask for help."

Level 1 "macro"	Forgiveness is unknown in Heaven, where peace abides and forgiving is not needed. Although not of God, it is the best illusion, leading us away from our mistakes and to God, as outlined in Level 2 below.
Level 2 "micro"	The ***process*** of forgiveness is the way that we: 1) correct our mistakes, 2) let go of ego and pain, 3) realize our eternal identity and invulnerability in God, 4) at last forgive ourselves and, 5) remember God.

Table 18.

Forgiveness According to Levels

(expanded from Wapnick 1989)

And second, we need to know *how* to ask God for help through whichever spiritual practice will best assist us, and practice the Course's teachings. Each time that we ask -- through prayer or another way -- we will usually experience a miracle and some forgiveness/letting go.

What we eventually learn and experience through forgiveness is that as *a perfect child of God* we are *invulnerable* and *eternal*. If we are invulnerable and eternal, then *what others do to us* and *we do to ourself* will have *no lasting* hurtful, harmful or detrimental *effect*. This spiritual fact is why we can safely forgive others for what "never happened," since what God created (i.e., us) is already and always perfect and unalterable.

Forgiveness then, is a process of seeing, understanding and experientially knowing that in my spirit/mind/consciousness I am invulnerable and that therefore no one can harm me in any way.

Forgiveness does not see or recognize sin. It lets go. It is still. And, quietly, it does nothing. It observes, waits, and does not judge. The Course says, "Do nothing, then, and let forgiveness show you what to do, through Him [the Holy Spirit] who is your Guide, your Savior and Protector, strong in hope, and certain of your ultimate success." (401W, 5:1)

The Course links miracles with forgiveness so closely that they are essentially the same experience. When we practice miracles we feel the peace of forgiveness, and vice versa. That is why the more we practice miracles, the easier it becomes to let go of our conflicts and their associated painful feelings that occur in the natural evolution of our relationships with self, others and God.

CHARACTERISTICS OF FORGIVENESS

Like other spiritual terms and experiences, forgiveness has several characteristics which I list in Table 19 on the next page. Forgiveness is a gradual and internal process started by and in our mind each time that we choose God and thereby co-create miracles. Once our mind (our decision maker) initiates and activates it, the Holy Spirit does the rest. Committed to our choice for God, we can then sit back and relax. Forgiveness is a gentle shift, change or transformation within a conflicted and painful, special (unholy) relationship. This shift usually occurs when the goals and experience of that painful relationship are made by our mind and the Holy Spirit into that of a now holy and peaceful relationship.

Forgiveness is basically an acquired and learned letting go of our ego and its associated pain. It bridges the gap between perception and truth, and is ultimately brought about by the Holy Spirit.

Acquired, learned	**Our only meaningful function and responsibility**
Letting go of ego	**World's equivalent of Heaven's justice**
Joining in holy relationship	**Based in communication**
Similar to miracles, salvation, Atonement and the holy instant	**Messenger of love** **Brings healing**
A gradual process started in the mind and carried out by Holy Spirit	**Shifts the focus on differentness to sameness (unity, oneness)**
Holy Spirit's function	**Helps us see and experience the real world**
Holy Spirit teaches forgiveness and uses it to heal	**Willingness that the truth be true**
Looking beyond error	**Answer to attack**
Release from illusion	**The end of specialness**
Healing of the perception of separation	**Way we remember God**
Realize nothing to forgive	**The key to happiness**
Offers miracles **Induces the holy instant**	**Temporary, not the end (God does the rest)**

Table 19.

Some Characteristics of Forgiveness from ACIM

Forgiveness thus brings about healing. This healing occurs primarily within the mind and experience of the individual person or soul (mind/spirit/consciousness) who has chosen God and thus forgiveness. Like the miracle, forgiveness *undoes* or removes our attachment to our ego and the pain which that generates. It then outshines and translates these into the truth of God's love and peace. Forgiveness reverses the steps that the ego had us take originally and that we unknowingly repeat over and over until we find "a better way." Miracles and forgiveness are thus a letting go of our attitude of conflict and experience of pain.

* * *

The real world of *God's Love* and p*eace* were there *within us* all along. When we made and chose our ego, we lost our awareness of God's Love and peace within us. By choosing God when we are in the pain of each of our conflicts, we can now let go of our ego and re-experience peace.

This choice between God and the ego is not new. Some guise of it has been described by many spiritual teachers over the last three thousand or more years. What the Course has done that is new and expansive is to present this choice more clearly, deeply and comprehensively that now makes it easier for us to grasp in a practical and experiential way. The Course's messages of miracles and forgiveness are one of its most useful teachings.

What could there be to fear in a world that I have forgiven, that has forgiven me?

A Course in Miracles p 99T

---

18 Forgiveness: Part Two

The Course says that miracles are natural signs of forgiveness. But how can we make that information useful in our lives? While it is hard to describe our meaningful personal experiences in words, as an example of the forgiveness process I will summarize some of what I experienced when I faced a long conflict with my biological father.

Forgiving My Father

It took me almost the first forty years of my life to realize that I grew up in a dysfunctional family. My parents mistreated and neglected us (me, my sister and brother) as kids. After that realization, I worked on my own healing and, as a physician and therapist, assisted others in theirs. In that whole process I learned a lot.

I eventually talked to my mother and shared my realizations and feelings about our troubled family, and was pleasantly surprised that she acknowledged that it happened. With humility, she said that she had not been a good mother to us, and apologized for it. We talked about it all for an hour or so, and then again off and on over the next few years. I've felt much better about it since then.

Each time that I tried to talk to my father about it, he got angry and raged at me. When he did that, the feelings I felt the most were fear, shame, confusion and hurt. Eventually, I got angry and decided that to protect myself from further hurt I needed some healthy boundaries with him. I began to avoid talking to him and being around him.

Finally, I wrote him a letter about how I was feeling, which was basically a request that he be real with me. He rejected it and blamed it on my mother, but would never talk to me about my letter. He and I remained mostly alienated from each other and he died 15 years ago.

Just before he died, I learned that during his marriage to my mother he had been in an affair with another woman for the last 25 years of his life and had fathered a child with her. To top it all off, I also discovered that when he died he left his entire estate of about $220,000 to this woman and their daughter, and left a dollar to each of us, his legitimate children. He had just divorced our mother a few months before he died, when they were both in their mid-eighties.

This left me with a lot of hurt and anger, and I had a hard time grieving it and his death.

In the few years since he died I tried to pray for him and me, but I still felt the hurt and anger, which I often expressed to people I could talk to about it. Studying the Course has inspired me to let him go. While I'd long known that he was a wounded person himself and was probably incapable of being a healthy father (or husband to our mother), I began to learn from the Course how my true essence as a child of God was invulnerable.

I eventually have come to realize, after years of hard work as a recovering person, that he didn't actually hurt me in a lasting way. In fact, in a strange sort of way I can even feel some degree of gratitude that he did what he did (and didn't do). Without it, I would not have healed as I have and written what I have, including Healing the Child Within *and these two books on the Course*

I never really knew our father. He couldn't be real with me, and I had a hard time being real with him. Over the years I've come to let him go slowly. The Course, prayer, miracles and God have been essential in my process of healing. Whether I call what happened forgiveness or by some other name may not matter to me as much as knowing that I'm experiencing some peace now about it all.

Overall, what happened for me was that I first had to try to heal some of my Stage Zero disorders (see Table 5 on page 46). Then I had to heal at an even deeper level in an extended Stage Two recovery program. During much of this time I studied the Course, but I got out of it only what I was ready for. At that time I was not ready or able to work at a deeper spiritual level, which I call Stage Three recovery or healing, because I didn't know my true self (Child Within) well enough to begin to differentiate that real me from the false me (ego). Having completed much of that Stage Two healing, I've been able to use the Course at a deeper level. Now experientially realizing that I am a child of God, I've been able to understand what the Course is saying about our spiritual identity, the journey to God, and forgiveness.

In the rest of this chapter I will describe some more about what I understand that the Course is saying about the process of forgiveness.

THE PROCESS OF FORGIVENESS

Wapnick (1997) has described three steps that the Course enumerates in the process of forgiveness (in 1987 Robert Perry also offered a similar version of these steps). The first two of these steps *we* do, and the third we *let God* do, as shown in Table 20. While the Course describes each of these steps from many angles throughout its pages, I offer a summary of them as follows.

FIRST

The first step is the most difficult. This is because at first it may be hard to see that we made our ego and chose it (ego attachment), which offers us "salvation" through separation and projection of our pain onto others (in special relationships). The Course describes this *unconscious process of self-harm* in many ways, perhaps the simplest of which is the statement that "...you are doing this unto yourself." (587T, 10:1)

But with repeated failure, we may become frustrated. Eventually, we may begin to search, and then find another way. That way can be by experimenting with choosing God and simply observing what happens within our inner life. It can be here that we awaken spiritually even more.

1) **Realize** that **I cause my own pain**.
2) At feeling any pain, **choose God**
3) **Let God** do the rest

Table 20.

Three Steps of Forgiveness

(from ACIM & Wapnick 1997)

Eventually, through trial and error, we can begin to discover that the cause of our pain is in our own mind. The Course says, "If you will recognize that all the attack you perceive is in your own mind and nowhere else, you will at last have placed its source, and where it begins it must end." (223T,10:1). If I (as my mind) can solve my problem and salve my pain, then I (as my mind) caused it by believing my attacker could hurt me.

In the Twelve Steps of AA and other self-help fellowships, this step of the forgiveness process is roughly equivalent to their Steps number 1, 4, 5, 8, 9, and 10 (see Twelve Steps on page 22).

SECOND

The next step of forgiveness is usually easier than the first one. The problem with it is that in the middle of conflict and pain we are often so ego-involved and otherwise unconscious that we do not know that we have any other choice. We forgot. So our task at this point is to *remember* or realize that *we have a choice* for God. We remember God, and then make our choice. Choosing God is similar to the Twelve Steps 2, 3, 6, 7, and 11. We can do so by saying a prayer, in meditation, or by using another spiritual practice that works for us. We simply remember and then choose God.

In the section of Chapter 31 of the Text titled "Choose Once Again," the Course says, "Trials are but lessons that you failed to learn presented once again, so where you made a faulty choice before you now can make a better one, and thus escape all pain that what you chose before has brought to you. In every difficulty, all distress, and each perplexity Christ calls to you and gently says, 'My brother, choose again.' " (666T,3:1-2)

FINAL

The final step of forgiveness is to do what Twelve Step programs refer to as "Let go and let God." This step is not ours to do, except for our surrendering and letting go so that God can do the rest. The Course sometimes refers to this step as "I need do nothing." Here and now I simply let go and let God.

Chapter 18 of the Text says that when we ask God for help, we transform a painful special relationship into a holy one and thereby experience more peace. This experience of peace comes with the happy realization that "I need do nothing." (389T,5:1-7)

"Here is the ultimate release which everyone will one day find in his own way, at his own time. ...To do nothing is to rest, and make a place within you where the activity of the body ceases to demand attention. Into this place the Holy Spirit comes, and there abides. He will remain when you forget, and the body's activities return to occupy your conscious mind." (389T,6:1; 390T,7:7-9)

*   *   *

The process of forgiveness is no more or less than repeating or continuing a string of our self-initiating several to many miracles. And we experience each miracle by choosing God. In especially difficult times we may have to choose God one minute or even one second at a time.

Throughout its pages the Course describes the same experience - miracles - from different perspectives, including forgiveness, salvation, Holy Instant, oneness and Atonement. Through the mind's correction called the miracle, forgiveness is the undoing of the ego's debilitating principles of denial and projection.

Forgiveness is the key to happiness.

A Course in Miracles p 268T

---

19 Forgiving Myself

We learn to forgive others in part so that we can learn to forgive ourselves. We project our conflicts (especially shame, guilt and fear) onto others, and by forgiving them, eventually we see that we can forgive ourselves for what is ultimately our own self-harm. While others may have also mistreated or neglected us, most of our pain came from our own misunderstandings about reality when we bought the ego's line that we were bad, which the Course calls guilt and we can also call toxic shame.

The ego told us that if denial of our pain didn't work, then projecting it onto others would decrease it. In his book *The Message of A Course in Miracles* (1997) Wapnick describes the ego's insane perception as constituting our "three selves," as outlined in Table 21 on the next page.

According to Wapnick's understanding of the Course, Self **A** takes on its own ego's shame (I'm bad). It then projects its own accepted shame onto another person (Self **C**) (you're bad for victimizing me), following which it feels like C's victim (Self **B**). Miracles and forgiveness invite the Holy Spirit to shift that mistaken thinking for us into God's truth, which establishes that: **A'**- I'm a sinless child of God, **B'**- I'm innocent, and **C'** You and others are innocent.

* * *

In its teachings, the Course does not tell us what to do in the specific case of active child abuse or other trauma. But it does tell us that we do not need to crucify ourselves (52T,3:1-11; 94T,11:2), which I interpret would mean that *we do not need to expose ourselves to unnecessary pain.* In the New Testament Jesus said, "Don't cast your pearls among swine." When we experience ongoing abuse of any kind, I believe we can set healthy boundaries with any offender, which I describe in *Boundaries and*

Relationships, and then use the principles of the Course when we choose. If we do that, and ask God/Holy Spirit/Christ for guidance and assistance, we will likely find our right direction as well.

Ego's Insane Perception	***Shift/Healing***	***God's Truth***
A - I'm bad: self-hatred, guilt/toxic shame; projected onto you (C)	***From the miracle/forgiveness: We're both innocent***	**A' - I'm a sinless child of God**
B - I'm a martyr/victim		**B' - I'm innocent**
C -You're bad for victimizing me; projected onto you, *my special relationship*		**C' - You and others are innocent**

Table 21.

Our " Three Selves "

(expanded from Wapnick's view of the Course 1997)

Some people may believe that forgiveness is accomplished by sheer will or determination. They may believe that once they have initiated these, all they have to do is say, "I forgive you!" and as if by magic, all their conflict and pain is supposed to dissolve. If that were true, most people would have a lot less pain. In my own experience, when I've tried to forgive someone this way, it didn't work. But when I've used the Course's teachings, it's usually worked.

I end this Chapter and the body of this book with two paragraphs from the Preface of the Course that summarize forgiveness as well as any I have seen (p xiii of the Course).

"Forgiveness is unknown in Heaven, where the need for it would be inconceivable. However, in this world forgiveness is a necessary correction for all the mistakes that we have made. To offer forgiveness is the only way for us to have it, for it reflects the law of Heaven that giving and receiving are the same. Heaven is the natural state of all the Sons of God as He created them. Such is their reality forever. It has not changed because it has been forgotten.

"Forgiveness is the means by which we will remember. Through forgiveness the thinking of the world is reversed. The forgiven world becomes the gate of Heaven, because by its mercy we can at last forgive ourselves. Holding no one prisoner to guilt, we become free. Acknowledging Christ in all our brothers, we recognize His Presence in ourselves. Forgetting all our misperceptions, and with nothing from the past to hold us back, we can remember God. Beyond this learning cannot go. When we are ready, God Himself will take the final step in return to Him."

From studying the Course and practicing its principles, I have realized that forgiveness is not an ideal. Rather, it is a reality that is of great practical usefulness to us in remembering God and experiencing peace. We can experience forgiveness, which can also be called "letting go," and a miracle each time that we choose God over our ego.

Fear binds the world. Forgiveness sets it free.

A Course in Miracles p 58 T

Epilogue

Having read and studied the Course now for over 30 years, I've sometimes had an approach-avoidance relationship with it. At first I was drawn to it by curiosity, and then later by the peace that it promised and often gave me. But I was also repelled by two experiences. Early, I felt overwhelmed at times when reading it, which I now know was my scared and confused ego protesting. This discomfort lasted intermittently for only a few years, and since then has been essentially gone. I've also not been able to read it for more than a few paragraphs or pages at a time because of the concentrated nature of the material. This may be related to what a colleague said about the Course, that "Every sentence is pregnant with spiritual information."

For the last few years my relationship with the Course has been nearly all positive. As I've continued to read, study and sometimes teach it, I've tried to make more sense of it. Some of my favorite and useful sections have been the more "linear" ones, such as the "What is...?" sections (e.g., What is Forgiveness?, etc) in Part II of the Workbook and the Clarification of Terms section at the end of the Manual for Teachers. Inspired by these and by the questions of our students when Barbara and I teach about the Course, plus my own occasional frustration when studying the more circular sections, I have outlined the Course in this Bird's eye view.

I sense that for myself and for many readers the discomfort and frustration at times when reading and studying the Course may be a necessary component in our healing process. At the same time, I've seen how helpful it has been in experiencing miracles, forgiveness and peace when I and other students and teachers *improve* our *understanding* of the Course's teachings. And so I wrote this first volume: *Choosing God:* A Bird's eye view of *A Course in Miracles.*

TEACHERS OF GOD

When I finished Chapter 19 on "Forgiving Myself," I realized that I had several more topics to cover that are presented in the Course as being key information. Thus I end this volume here for sake of this book's size and timing of its publication. I title the next volume *Teachers of God:* Further Reflections on *A Course in Miracles,* wherein I will in a similar fashion describe my understanding of what the Course says about still more of its most important topics that due to space limits I was unable to include in this volume.

The Course says that we are all students and teachers of God. In the second volume I describe the **characteristics of God's teachers**, including Trust, Honesty, Tolerance, Gentleness, Joy, Defenselessness, Generosity, Patience, Faithfulness and Open-mindedness. I will also discuss other important topics such as **Healing**, the **Body** and the **World**, **Time**, **Sin, Innocence**, the **Dreamer** and the **Dream**, **Grandeur** and **Grandiosity**, the **Atonement**, **Prayer**, and the **Peace** of God.

I hope that this book has begun to give you a clearer understanding of the Course, which is the most spiritually exciting, nourishing, and useful book I have ever read. While the Course cannot be summarized or abridged, this book *Choosing God* may help you to focus more on reading and studying the words of *A Course in Miracles* itself. The message of its author, whom I call the living Christ, and others call Jesus, is contained in nearly every sentence and in the totality of its three volumes. The Course has helped me greatly, and I hope it will benefit you as well.

In love and peace,

Charles Whitfield
Atlanta, GA July 2010

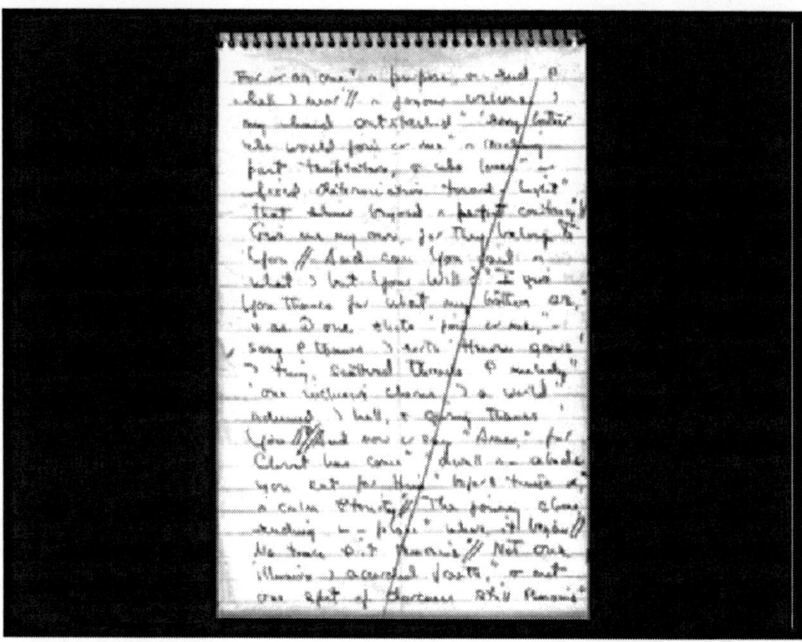

When the Voice said to Helen, "This is a Course in Miracles. Please take notes." Helen began writing in this fashion.

This is the first page of her notes

Appendix:

EVOLUTION OF THE VERSIONS OF THE COURSE - A SUMMARY

Course teacher and author Robert Perry reviews the evolution of the Course versions in a scholarly article on his website *www.circleofa.org* and which I summarize below.

Example Differences	***Urtext*** **Version**	***Hugh Lynn Cayce*** **Version**	***Standard*** **Course**
Date	**1972**		**1975/6. 1992/5**
Description	What Bill typed from Helen's shorthand notebooks 1965 to 72	Helen's retyping of the second draft.	Helen and Ken do the final editing ...
Dynamics and Layout	Continuous, without section or chapter breaks in the text. Capitalization, punctuation, and paragraphing are rough.	1972 A middle ground between the Urtext and the standard Course. She and Bill make the rough original dictation cleaner and more readable.	...and publish it with Judy Skutch of the Foundation for Inner Peace as the First (1976) and later Second (1992) Editions
Editors	Helen Schucman – scribe(transcriber)/editor Bill Thetford – typist/editor		Helen Schucman – scribe/editor Ken Wapnick - editor
Reasons	Birthing the Course.	Need to make the Course clearer and more reader friendly.	Appropriate need to make it reader friendly for the average person.

Table 22.

Versions of the Course

The Urtext – What Bill typed from Helen's shorthand notebooks 1965 to 72. The Voice Helen heard - Jesus - gave Helen and Bill instructions for editing the Course. He mentioned two kinds of changes: 1. ***Remove material intended for you*** (Helen and Bill) ***alone, e.g.,*** Jesus speaks about Helen and Bill's personal lives, relationships, interactions, and developmental issues, -- ***and***

2. Correct scribal errors, e.g., early in the dictation, Jesus often told Helen that she had heard him wrong, and then corrected what she had written, sometimes more than once. Most of these were corrected by Helen and Bill as per the instructions.

In the actual editing of the Urtext, Helen and Bill went beyond these two kinds of changes and also removed the following: psychological material (relating the Course to the thought systems of Freud, Jung, and Rank), discussion of various life issues (e.g., sex, homosexuality, selection of partners, the role of the teacher), religious and theological material (e.g., angels, reincarnation, karma, spirit possession, speaking in tongues, witchcraft) and miscellaneous specifics (e.g., the Holocaust, daylight saving time, the CIA, alcoholism, alchemy, money, voting).

Helen and Bill also moved over 6,000 words in the standard Course from their original location, largely because the miracle principles originally came interspersed with much unrelated and some related discussion. The flow of thought in the early sections is choppy. The material is more of a dialogue between Helen and Jesus than the monologue of the later Course. Jesus often spoke personally to them. Helen often interjected and Jesus responded, sometimes stepping in and correcting something Helen wrote down, saying she heard him wrong.

The major differences between the Urtext and the standard Course are mostly in the first four to nine chapters of the Text, and the amount of editing tapers off gradually. According to Andrew Allansmith, Helen, Bill and later with Ken Wapnick deleted an overall of about 48,000 words from the Urtext into the standard Course. The deletions decrease until in

Chapter 9 only about 200 words are removed and in Chapter 10 only 37 words are removed. Helen then retyped the Urtext and, according to Ken Wapnick, "edited as she went along," effectively producing a new version, which Wapnick calls "the second draft." Some suspect that the Urtext currently available on the Internet is actually a combination of the Urtext and the second draft, available online since 2004. To get the full account I suggest reading Perry's clear article at circleofa.org. To order a copy of the original Urtext as the actual copy of the typewritten pages from Bill Thetford's typewriter with Jesus' original dictation from Helen's notebook that includes 60 pages of "special messages," on 1800 pages with Helen and Bill's occasional handwritten edits, contact Andrew Allansmith at ACIM Urtext, 17197 Laurel Road, Los Gatos, CA 95033 or see *spiritualear.org/urtext.html* or call him at 408-353-3451.

Hugh Lynn Cayce Version - named after the son of the famous psychic Edgar Cayce. Hugh Lynn had been supportive of Helen throughout her scribing of the Course, and in 1972 she and Bill sent him a somewhat edited copy of the completed Urtext version. They called this the Hugh Lynn Version and it has become popularly known as that or HLC. The HLC occupies a middle ground between the Urtext and the standard Course: Most of the personal and professional material is removed and references to Helen and Bill are deleted. Chapter and section breaks are inserted in the Text. Capitalization, punctuation, and paragraphing are cleaned up some. The flow of thought in early parts is smoothed out. About 1,000 words are moved and placed elsewhere. The HLC version of the Text is available as the **Original Edition** from the Course in Miracles Society, 7602 Pacific Street, Ste 304, Omaha, NB 68114 and *www.jcim.net.*

Standard Course - In 1973, Helen showed the Course to Ken Wapnick, who said: "I commented to Helen and Bill that I thought the manuscript needed some additional editing. Some of the personal and professional material still remained, and seemed inappropriate for a published edition. The first four chapters did not read well at all, in large part because the deleted personal material left gaps in the remaining text, and thus required minor word additions to smooth the transition. Also, some of the divisions in the material appeared arbitrary to me, and many of the section and chapter titles did not really coincide with the material....Finally, the paragraphing, punctuation, and capitalization were not only idiosyncratic, but notoriously inconsistent.

"Helen and Bill agreed that it did need a final run-through. As Bill lacked the patience and attention to detail that was needed for such a task, we decided that Helen and I should go through it together....I earlier quoted Helen's statement that she had come to think of *A Course in Miracles* as her life's work, and she approached the editing project with a real dedication. She and I meticulously went over every word to be sure that the final manuscript was right."

When Helen and Ken finished, they had edited as much beyond the HLC as the HLC was beyond the Urtext; e.g., 1) They changed some of the chapter, section breaks and titles; 2) Plus paragraphing, punctuation, and capitalization. 3) They removed more personal and professional material, now resulting in removing a total of 48,000 personal words regarding Helen and Bill and other words from the Urtext.

This result was the standard Course first printed in 1975 as what is now called the [Eleanor] Criswell Edition [who was asked by Judy Skutch to print 300 copies by EC's Free Person Press], and then published in **1976** as the **First Edition** (the versions recently released from copyright in the court case described below). In between these two printings, in the fall of 1975 Helen scribed the Clarification of Terms which they added to the Teachers Manual. This First Edition is no longer bound by copyright as explained below.

Second Edition - Published in 1992 by the Foundation for Inner Peace. In the introduction to a pamphlet entitled ***Errata for the Second Edition of 'A Course in Miracles***,' Ken Wapnick summarizes that the evolving Course manuscript had gone through several retypings before it was finally printed. Helen had twice retyped the Text (the second being the HLC) and "none of these retypings was ever proofread." Helen and Ken's edit of the Text was again retyped twice before printing. Because these retypings were "also not adequately proofread," some material was inadvertently omitted. Furthermore, some typographical errors went unnoticed. Thus, when the Second Edition of the Course was undertaken it seemed to be an appropriate time to insert the deleted material and correct all prior mistakes. To ensure that this Second Edition be as free as possible from errors, the three books of the First Edition were proofread against the Urtext that Bill had originally typed from Helen's notes, they consulted all retypings, as well as Helen's original shorthand notebooks, to trace the found errors and omissions.

The Second Edition, therefore, contains 97 sentences and six complete paragraphs that had inadvertently fallen out along the way. The Second Edition also contains a numbering system for sections, paragraphs, and sentences, which was not in the First Edition. This is the version that most readers have now.

My Personal Use: I have most versions. In about 1977 I bought the First Edition, read it at least twice, and then The Song of Prayer and Psychotherapy (both now included in the Third edition). Then in the 1980s heard the audio version several times read by Kelly Love, viewed the videotape of The Forgotten Song and The Song Remembered at least 8 times, in the early 1990s read the Second Edition several times and began writing these books after 1996. Then obtained the HLC and Urtext.

In his clear and more detailed description, **Robert Perry** notes that the sheer volume of line-by-line editing may take one aback, as we are accustomed to thinking of the words of the Course as being straight from Jesus. The following Table example on the next page will give you a sense of the line-by-line editing. I suggest you read it in two ways. First, read down each column. Then, read across -reading each line as it evolves through the different versions.

Urtext	***Hugh Lynn Cayce***	***Standard Course***
You now share my inability	As you share my inability	As you share my unwillingness
to tolerate the lack of love	to tolerate lack of love	to accept error
in yourself and in everyone else,	in yourself and others,	in yourself and others,
and must join	you must join	you must join
the Great Crusade to correct it.	the Great Crusade to correct it.	the great crusade to correct it;
The slogan for this Crusade is "Listen, Learn, and *Do*."	The slogan for the Crusade is "Listen, learn, and *do*;"—	
This means Listen to My Voice,	Listen to my voice,	listen to my voice,
Learn to undo the error,	learn to undo error,	learn to undo error
and *do* something to correct it.	and *do* something to correct it.	and act to correct it.

Table 23.

Second Edition alterations to the text

In 2004 the mass market paperback was published and in 2007 the 3rd edition of the Course came. An excellent summary of how the Course developed from a personal perspective with Helen and Bill as experienced by Ken Wapnick and Judy Skutch is available in a two DVD pair as ***Memories of Helen and Bill*** from the Foundation for Inner Peace (ACIM.org).

Brief Controversy on the Course's Copyright

Beginning in the early 1990's, the enforcement of the copyright of *A Course in Miracles* by its copyright holders (the Foundation for Inner Peace, the Foundation for A Course in Miracles, and Penguin) grew increasingly restrictive, which led to lawsuits. One of these suits was filed in 1996 by the copyright holders against the First Christian Church of Full Endeavor (also known as Endeavor Academy) saying that Endeavor had violated their copyright on the Course by publishing large parts of it without their consent. The defendants said that their copyright for *A Course in Miracles* was invalid.

After seven years, on October 24 2003 Judge Robert Sweet of the Southern District Court of New York ruled that the copyright of the First Edition of *A Course in Miracles* was invalid. He gave the copyright holders time to appeal the decision, and they chose not to. The copyright on the First Edition of the Course was thereby officially revoked for good. (The copyrights for the Second Edition and the "Clarification of Terms" remain legally valid.) See Robert Perry's commentary on what the final verdict means for the future of the Course, and read his article entitled And Now It Belongs to the World and Rev. Tony Ponticello's article on circleofa.org entitled The Copyright.

References

Anonymous: *A Course in Miracles*. Foundation for Inner Peace, First edition 1975/6, Second edition 1992 *Foundation for A Course in Miracles* (Viking Penguin), NY, l996

Anonymous: Psychotherapy: Purpose, Process and Practice. (Booklet). Foundation for Inner Peace, Tiburon, CA. l976

Berke D: *Love Always Answers:* Walking the path of miracles. Crossroad, NY, 1994

Findisen B: *ACIM Concordance* to Volume One: Text. Coleman Graphics, Farmingdale, NY, 1983

Foundation for Inner Peace The Story of A Course in Miracles Mill Valley, CA *www.acim.org*

Funk RW and The Jesus Seminar: *The Gospel of Jesus*: According to the Jesus Seminar. Polebridge Press 1999

Lazaris: Releasing negative ego (taped talk). Concept Synergy, Palm Beach, Fl, 1986

Jyoti and Russell Park, Center for Sacred Studies, California. Ambassador to the International Council of 13 Indigenous Grandmothers, dedicated to peace and unity for all people. *www.sacredstudies.org*

Metzger BM, Coogan MD (eds): *The Oxford Companion to the Bible*. Oxford University Press, NY, 1993

Mundy J: *Awaken to Your Own Call:* Exploring ACIM. Crossroad, NY, l994

Mundy J: *Time, Death and A Course in Miracles.* Prints of Peace, Monroe, NY, 1975

Perry R: *Reality & Illusion*: An overview of Course metaphysics. Part 1. The Circle of Atonement, Sedona, AZ 1993

Perry R: *Path of Light:* Stepping into Peace with *A Course in Miracles.* Circle Publishing, Sedona, AZ 2004

Perry R: Return to the Heart of God: The Practical Philosophy of A Course in Miracles. The Circle of Atonement , Sedona, AZ 2007

Skutch R: *Journey Without Distance:* The story behind *A Course in Miracles*. Celestial Arts, Berkeley, CA 1984

Sylvest VM: *The Formula* Sunstar Publishing Ltd. Fairfield, IA l996

Vahle N: *A Course in Miracles: The Lives of Helen Schucman and William Thetford*. Open View Press 2009

Vaughan F, Walsh R: *Accept This Gift.* Tarcher/Perigee Books. New York, NY 1983

Watson A: *Seeing the Bible Differently.* The Circle of Atonement , Sedona, AZ 1997

Wapnick K: *Concordance* of *A Course in Miracles*. Foundation for Inner Peace 1997

Wapnick K: *The Fifty Miracle Principles* of "A Course in Miracles": A Commentary on the Text, pages 1-4. Foundation for ACIM l985

Wapnick K: *Absence from Felicity*: The Story of Helen Schucman and Her Scribing of A Course in Miracles. Foundation for ACIM l99l

Wapnick K: *A Vast Illusion*: Time according to ACIM. Foundation for ACIM, l990

Wapnick K: Christian Psychology in ACIM (booklet). Foundation for Inner Peace, Mill Valley, CA l976

Wapnick K: *Glossary Index for ACIM.* 3rd ed. Foundation for *ACIM* 1989

Wapnick, K: *The Message of A Course in Miracles.* vols. 1 and 2. Foundation for ACIM 1997

Wapnick K: Talks on ACIM. Silver Spring, MD about 1982, and Psychiatric Institute of Washington continuing education workshop about 1988

Wapnick G: quoted in Davies TL: Interview with Kenneth and Gloria Wapnick. *Love and Forgiveness* 1:2 (March/April), p.23, 1997

Wapnick K: Scriptural Index for *A Course in Miracles.* 2006 An index of more than 800 scriptural references found in the Course, cross-referenced to the Bible

Wapnick K, Skutch Whitson J. *Memories of Helen and Bill.* Foundation for Inner Peace, Mill Valley, CA www.acim.org

Whitfield BH: *Spiritual Awakenings.* Health Communications, Deerfield Beach, FL l995

Whitfield BH: *The Natural Soul:* Unity with the Spiritual Energy that connects us. Muse House Press, Atlanta, 2010

Whitfield CL: Chapter 65. Co-dependence, addictions, and related disorders. in Lowinson, et al (eds): *Substance Abuse*: A Comprehensive Textbook. 3rd edition, Williams & Wilkins, Baltimore, 1997 (also in Second Edition, l992)

Whitfield CL, Whitfield BH, Prevatt J, Park R: *The Power of Humility*: Choosing Peace over Conflict in Relationships. Health Communications, Deerfield Beach, FL, 2006 -- Refers to the Course often

Whitfield CL (in process for 2010 /or 11). *You May NOT be Mentally Ill*: Misdiagnosed and mistreated with drugs that don't work or make you worse. Muse House Press, Atlanta www.MuseHousePress.com

Whitfield CL : *Healing the Child Within*. Health Communications, Deerfield Beach, FL 1986

Whitfield CL: *A Gift to Myself*. Health Communications, Deerfield Bch, FL 1990

Whitfield CL: *Boundaries and Relationships*. Health Communications, Deerfield Bch, FL 1993

Whitfield CL: Spiritual energy: Perspectives from a map of the psyche and the Kundalini process In *Kundalini Rising:* Exploring the energy of awakening. Sounds True, Boulder CO 2009

Whitfield, B: Mental and emotional health and the Kundalini process. In *Kundalini Rising:* Exploring the energy of awakening. Sounds True, Boulder CO. 2009

Whitfield, B: *Final Passage:* Sharing the Journey as this life ends. Health Communications, Inc. Deerfield Bch, FL 1998

Williamson M: A *Return to Love*: Reflections on the principles of *A Course in Miracles.* HarperPerennial 1993

WEBSITES FOR MORE INFORMATION ON THE COURSE:

circleofa.org Circle Of Atonement ... honors the breadth and depth of the Course including radical, mind-expanding ideas as well as detailed instructions for practical application. ... grounded in long and close study of the Course and tested in personal experience.

www.facim.org Ken and Gloria Wapnick's informative website that presents the purpose and activities of the Foundation as well as what *A Course in Miracles*

www.acim.org website of the Foundation for Inner Peace, the original organization appointed by the scribe, Helen Schucman, to publish and distribute the only authorized manuscript of *A Course in Miracles*.

www.miraclesinactionpress.com/links.htm.

web.archive.org/web/20060128092110/www.miraclestudies.net/Biographical.html

www.facim.org/acim/glossary.htm -- Glossary on key Course terms from Ken Wapnick's website

About The Author

Charles L. Whitfield, MD, is a pioneer in addictions and in trauma recovery, including the way we remember childhood and other trauma and abuse. A physician and frontline therapist who assists trauma survivors in their healing, he is the author of over 65 published articles and 12 books, several of which are best sellers. He writes on trauma psychology, spirituality and recovery. ***Healing the Child Within*** and ***Boundaries and Relationships*** are classics in the field. Five of his books have been translated and published in eleven foreign languages.

Dr. Whitfield was one of the first physicians to teach about spirituality in recovery in a medical school setting. Since 1995 he has been voted by his peers as being one of the best doctors in America. For over 23 years he has taught at Rutgers University's Institute on Alcohol and Drug Studies. He recently was awarded their annual Lifetime Achievement Award by the Atlanta Therapeutic Professional Community.

He is a consultant and research collaborator at the Centers for Disease Control and Prevention since 1998 examining the aftereffects for adults that were repeatedly traumatized as children. He is a Fellow of The American Society for Addiction Medicine.

He has a private practice in Atlanta, Georgia, with his wife, Barbara, where they provide individual and group therapy for trauma survivors and people with addictions and other problems in living. He and Barbara have taught classes on ***A Course in Miracles*** and recently joined the faculty of the Center for Sacred Studies where they teach a module on Unity in Practice to graduating two year students becoming ordained as Ministers of Prayer. Together they serve as consulting editors for ***The Journal of Near-Death Studies*** and sit on the advisory board for The American Center for the Integration of Spiritually Transformational Experiences (ACISTE). For more information go to ***www.barbarawhitfield.com*** **and** ***www.cbwhit.com***

This interpretation presented in *Choosing God* reflects the understandings and experience of Charles L. Whitfield and others quoted and/or cited in the book and do not necessarily express the views of the Foundation for Inner Peace. The ideas represented herein are the personal interpretation and understanding of the author and are not endorsed by the copyright holder of *A Course in Miracles*®. I am grateful to the Foundation for Inner Peace for their permission to quote selected passages from *A Course in Miracles*. As suggested throughout this book, **I recommend** that each reader **refer to the Course itself** for its teachings, and not rely on my or others' interpretations.

A Course in Miracles is published by the **Foundation for Inner Peace**, P.O. Box 598, Mill Valley, CA 94942, and is copyrighted by the Foundation.

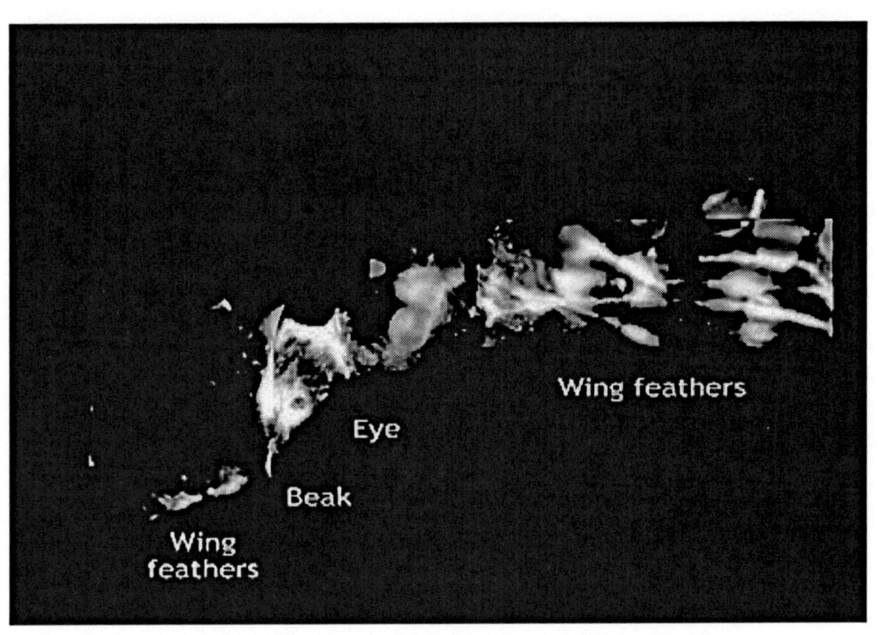

Imprint of white dove crashed onto glass
Catonsville, MD 1994

Index

A

B

C

D

E

F

G

H

I

J

K

L

M

N

O

P

Q

R

S

T

U

V

W

Y

This book is a continuation of Volume I, Choosing God: A Bird's Eye View of A Course in Miracles -- of this two volume pair.

In this book I pick up where the first book ended. Here I summarize 15 more key Course topics plus a new original chapter, The Universal Message of the Course in which I compare the Course to world religions and spiritual paths, including Alcoholics Anonymous and other Twelve Step Fellowships.

"Charles takes us into the heart and soul of A Course in Miracles"

Jyoti and Russell Park, PhD

Teachers of God

Further Reflections on

A Course in Miracles

Charles L Whitfield, MD

Author of Healing The Child Within

and

The Power of Humility

mhp

muse house press

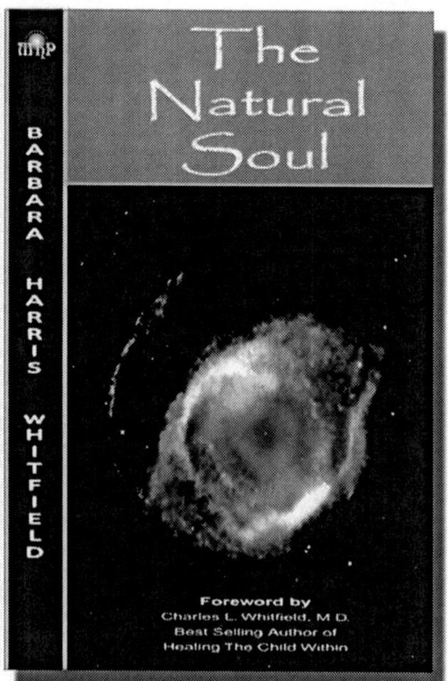

mhp
The Natural Soul
BARBARA HARRIS WHITFIELD
Foreword by
Charles L. Whitfield, M.D.
Best Selling Author of
Healing The Child Within

"So much has been written and said about the soul. In this book, we are shown the soul. Whitfield illustrated how to live from our soul and relate to the souls of others.

I have come to regard this book as a postcard from Whitfield's soul to ours, and my advice is to read it, say "thank you," and put it into practice."

Bruce Greyson, M.D.,

Chester F. Carlson Professor of Psychiatry and Neurobehavioral Sciences, University of Virginia School of Medicine

More from Muse House Press

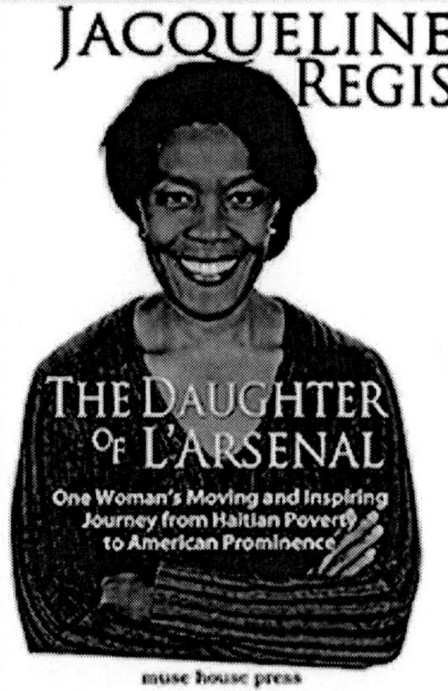

A inspiring story of a woman of two worlds. In this moving memoir of love and driven determination against all odds, Jacqueline Regis, an accomplished lawyer and judge, tells the story of her climb up from poverty in Haiti to prominence in America in vivid and stirring detail. She shares with us the hope and inspiration to keep reaching higher for our goals, and never giving in to anything less.

This book will inspire you to make the most of your life!

"...many tools and techniques to help the reader transform the ordinary difficulties of life into moments of calm, clarity and, sometimes, surprisingly, even the deepest joy. And they do it not only skillfully but with humor, too. This is a book to treasure --and to keep handy."

Kenneth Ring, PhD
Author of
Lessons from the Light

Look Inside

A Guide to Self-Awareness and Change

BARBARA HARRIS WHITFIELD AND SHARON K. CORMIER
Foreword by Charles L. Whitfield, MD

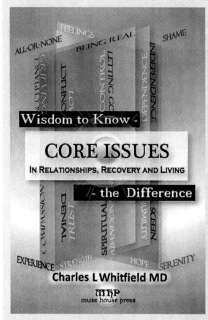

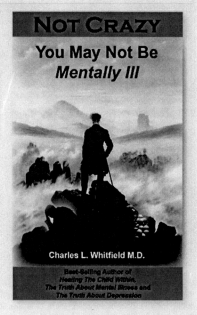

Other Helpful Books By *The Whitfields*

This is a landmark book by two long-time Moody Blues fans. In this book the Whitfields examine and bring to light the music and message of this great band of poets and musicians who have produced hit music for almost 50 years!.

In this book they explore:

*How they are unique among bands and music groups
*The nature of their musical magic and message
*How the Moodies' words and music work, song by song
*Why listening to their music raises our consciousness
*Why the Moodies have excelled for nearly five decades

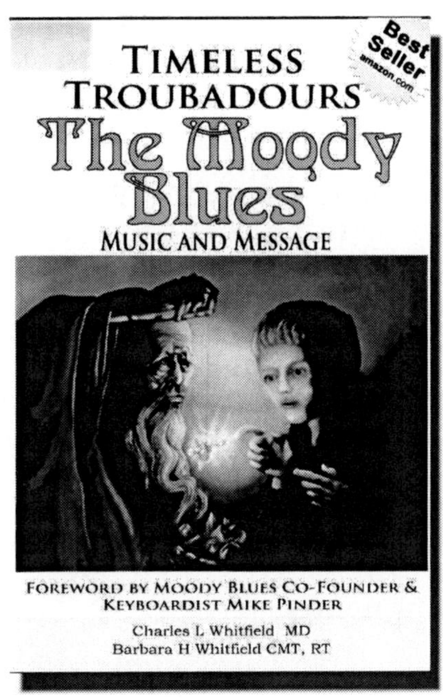

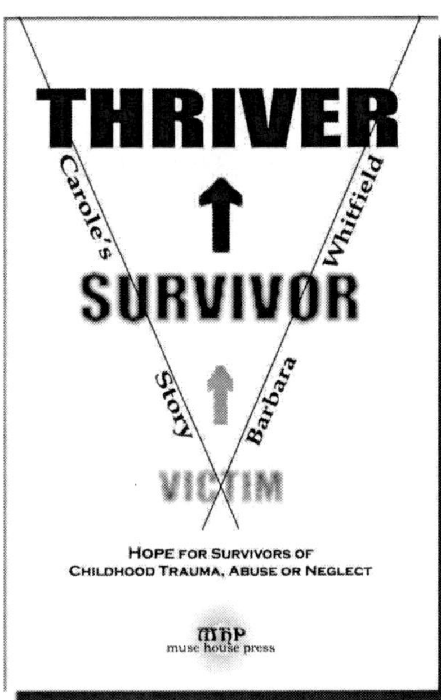

This is not an easy book to read. It contains real-life pain, sadness and loss. Some of us have suffered like Carole did --and worse-- yet in reading this book – we discover healing. There is help here. And most importantly, there is hope within these pages for anyone who has been severely and repeatedly traumatized, abused and/or neglected in childhood. Whitfield quotes from Carole's documentary: "The thunderstorms are just as beautiful as a sunny day. And so is life!"

—Donald Brennan
Certified Addiction Counselor
from the Foreword

OTHER HELPFUL BOOKS BY *CHARLES L. WHITFIELD, M.D.*

A Personal Workbook and Guide to the Best-Selling *Healing the Child Within*

In this book Dr. Whitfield continues and expands the ways to heal our Child Within which he began to describe in his best-selling Healing the Child Within. He presents specific guidelines and exercises for getting free of the chains of co-dependence and having grown up in a dysfunctional family.

HCI Book Review

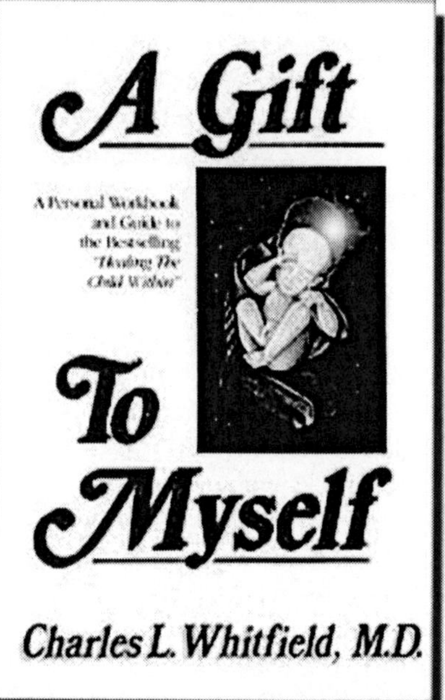

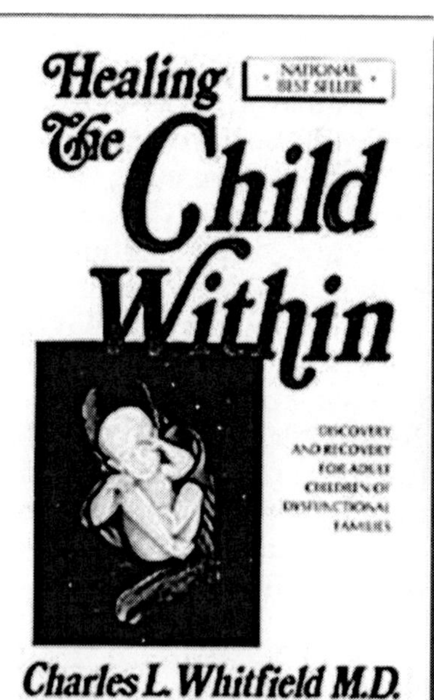

The
National Best-Seller!

"A concise, comprehensive and rather remarkable integration of the theory and practice of healing the child within; we highly recommend this useful book."

Herbert L. Gravitz, Ph.D.
Julie Bowden, MFCC

A Classic, Self-published, 1985

150 pages and 437 references on general and advanced spirituality that I wrote for my students at Rutgers University Advanced School of Alcohol and Drug Studies and elsewhere.

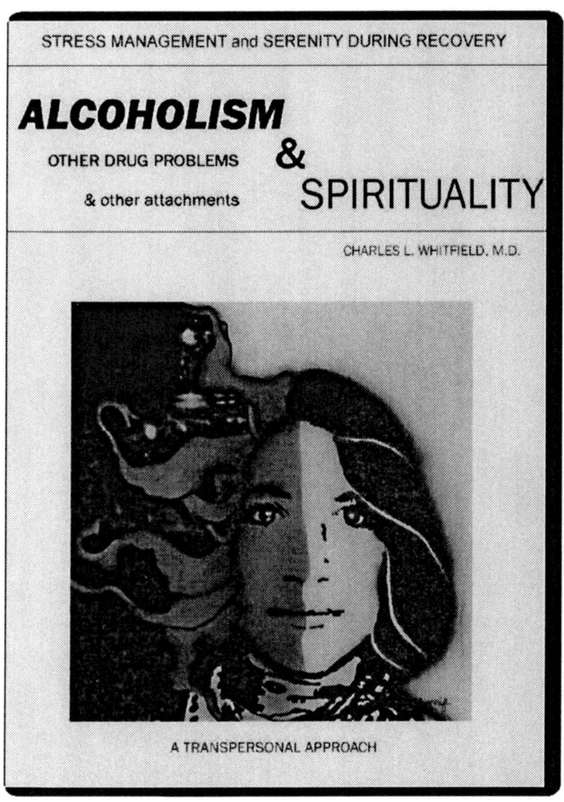

I have a few extra copies left from that printing available for $18.00 incl postage (other countries US$30, no personal checks) Send **money order** (preferred), PayPal (to cbwhit@comcast.net) or a good check to: Charles Whitfield

3462 Hallcrest Dr

Atlanta Ga 30319

Lightning Source UK Ltd.
Milton Keynes UK
UKOW02f1600010316

269384UK00002B/334/P